DEBBIE BROWN'S

Party Cakes

Debbie Brown's Party Cakes

HAMLYN

Thank you Mum

All photographs specially taken by Hilary Moore, except for the following, which were
provided by the Reed Consumer Books Picture Library:
David Jordan: 11,
Peter Myers: 9, 16, 17A, 18,
Clive Streeter: 7, 13, 15, 19, 23.

First published in Great Britain 1993
by Hamlyn an imprint of Reed Consumer Books Limited
Michelin House, 81 Fulham Road, London, SW3 6RB
and Auckland, Melbourne, Singapore and Toronto

ISBN 0 600 57738 4

Produced by Mandarin Offset
Printed and bound in Hong Kong

Editor: Isobel Holland
Art Editor: Lisa Tai
Production Controller: Sarah Rees
Jacket and Special photography: Hilary Moore
Special photography on pages 36, 42 and 82: Clive Streeter

Contents

Basic Cakes

These cake recipes are used throughout the book. To make it easier to follow, the ingredients are set out in chart form with cake sizes indicated by numbers.

MADEIRA CAKE

Madeira cake has a moist texture, yet is firm enough for novelty cakes which require a lot of cutting and shaping.

PREPARATION TIME: about 15 minutes
COOKING TIME: see chart
OVEN: 160°C, 325°F, Gas mark 3

1 Grease the bakeware, line the base and sides with greaseproof paper and grease again.

2 Cream the butter and sugar until light, fluffy and very pale.

3 Sift the flours together. Beat the eggs into the creamed mixture, one at a time, following each with a spoonful of flour.

4 Fold the remaining flour into the creamed mixture, followed by the grated lemon rind.

5 Turn into the prepared bakeware and level the top. Bake in a preheated oven for the time suggested in the chart or until well risen, firm to the touch and golden brown.

6 Cool in the bakeware for about 10 minutes, then turn out on to a wire rack and leave until cold. Do not peel off the lining paper, but wrap the cake in foil or store in an airtight container for at least 12 hours before cutting.

Right above: Madeira cake; right below: Victoria sponge cake

MADEIRA CAKE

★ LAZY DAYS ★ CHAMPAGNE ★ CHEF ★ CLOCK ★ CLOWN ★ DOLL ★ GOLF BAG ★
★ OFFICE ★ BLUE BUNNY ★ SHOE ★ TEDDY ★ TEENAGER ★ WITCH ★

	25 CM (10 INCH) SQUARE TIN	20 x 30 CM (8 x 12 INCH) OBLONG TIN	15 CM (6 INCH) ROUND TIN	1.2 LITRE (2 PINT) BOWL	2 x 8 CM (3½ INCH) DIAMETER BOWL	7 CM (3 INCH) DIAMETER MUG
SIZE	1	2	3	4	5	6
butter or margarine	350g (12oz)	350g (12oz)	175g (6oz)	150g (5oz)	50g (2oz)	40g (1½oz)
caster sugar	350g (12oz)	350g (12oz)	175g (6oz)	150g (5oz)	50g (2oz)	40g (1½oz)
self-raising flour	350g (12oz)	350g (12oz)	175g (6oz)	150g (5oz)	50g (2oz)	40g (1½oz)
plain flour	175g (6oz)	175g (6oz)	75g (3oz)	65g (2½oz)	25g (1oz)	25g (1oz)
eggs	6 (size 2)	6 (size 2)	3 (size 2)	2 (size 1)	1 (size 2)	1 (size 4)
grated lemon rind	2 lemons	2 lemons	1 lemon	½ lemon	¼ lemon	¼ lemon
cooking time	1-1¼ hours	1 hour	1-1¼ hours	1 hour	35 minutes	35 minutes

VICTORIA SPONGE CAKE

A classic, light Victoria sponge mixture, which tastes extra rich when made with butter.

PREPARATION TIME: about 30 minutes
COOKING TIME: see chart
OVEN: 190°C, 375°F, Gas mark 5

1 Grease the bakeware and either dust with flour or line the base with greaseproof paper and grease again.

2 Cream the butter and sugar until light, fluffy and very pale, then beat in the vanilla flavouring.

3 Beat in the eggs, one at a time, following each with a spoonful of the self-raising flour.

4 Sift the remaining flour and fold it very gently into the mixture alternately with the water.

5 Turn into the prepared bakeware and level the top. Bake in a preheated oven for the time suggested in the chart or until well risen and firm to the touch. Turn out on to a wire rack and leave to cool.

QUICK MIX CAKE

This is a very simple cake to prepare and bake. It is moist and light but with a firm enough texture to allow for the cutting and shaping required.

PREPARATION TIME: about 5 minutes
COOKING TIME: see chart
OVEN: 160°C, 325°F; Gas mark 3

1 Grease the bakeware and dust with a little flour.

2 Put the butter, sugar, eggs, sifted flour, baking powder and vanilla flavouring into a large bowl.

3 Mix the ingredients together with a wooden spoon or hand-held electric mixer, then beat vigorously for 1-2 minutes until the mixture is smooth and glossy.

4 Turn into the prepared bakeware and level the top. Bake in a preheated oven for the time suggested in the chart or until risen and firm to touch.

5 Cool in the bakeware for about 10 minutes, then turn out on to a wire rack. When cold, store in an airtight container or wrap in foil and leave for at least 12 hours before cutting.

*V*ICTORIA SPONGE CAKE

★ MOUSE PICNIC ★ THREE-TIER TEDDY ★

SIZE	20 CM (8 INCH) SQUARE TIN	18 CM (7 INCH) ROUND TIN	12 CM (5 INCH) ROUND TIN AND 7 CM (3 INCH) DIAMETER MUG
	1	2	3
butter or margarine	225g (8oz)	175g (6oz)	125g (4oz)
caster sugar	225g (8oz)	175g (6oz)	125g (4oz)
vanilla flavouring	4 drops	3 drops	2 drops
eggs (size 1 or 2)	4	3	2
self-raising flour	225g (8oz)	175g (6oz)	125g (4oz)
cold water	1 tablespoon	1 tablespoon	2 teaspoons
cooking time	50 minutes	40 minutes	35 minutes (large cake) 20 minutes (small cake)

For the 12 cm (5 inch) and 7 cm (3 inch) top tiers of the teddy cake, divide the mixture between the two containers by filling the mug about a third to half full, then placing the rest of the mixture in the 12 cm (5 inch) tin. Bake together, but remove the mug from the oven after 20 minutes and give the small tin an extra 15 minutes or so. This also applies to Healthy Sponge Cake size 4.

QUICK MIX CAKE

★ LAZY DAYS ★ LORRY ★ PUPPY ★ SHOE ★ WITCH ★

	20 CM (8 INCH) ROUND TIN	20 x 30 CM (8 x 12 INCH) OBLONG TIN	25 CM (10 INCH) SQUARE TIN	1.2 LITRE (2 PINT) BOWL	600 ML (1 PINT) BOWL
Size	1	2	3	4	5
butter or margarine	350g (12oz)	350g (12oz)	275g (10oz)	175g (6oz)	125g (4oz)
caster sugar	350g (12oz)	350g (12oz)	275g (10oz)	175g (6oz)	125g (4oz)
eggs (size 1 or 2)	6	6	5	3	2
self-raising flour	350g (12oz)	350g (12oz)	275g (10oz)	175g (6oz)	125g (4oz)
baking powder	–	3 teaspoons	2½ teaspoons	1½ teaspoons	1 teaspoon
vanilla flavouring	12 drops	12 drops	10 drops	6 drops	4 drops
cooking time	1½ hours	1-1¼ hours	1-1¼ hours	1-1¼ hours	50 minutes

Above: Quick mix cake

HEALTHY SPONGE CAKE

Carrots and apples add sweetness as well as giving a really moist texture to this cake. Make sure you use sweet eating apples when making this cake, such as Red Delicious, Royal Gala or Cox's Orange Pippins; when in season, these apples have a richer more delicious flavour. Because vegetable oil is used rather than butter or margarine, the mixture combines very quickly, making it a truly simple and easy cake for anyone to try. It offers a tasty and healthy alternative which is versatile enough to take either the butter cream or the fondant icing needed to make the cakes in this book. The nuts too, are important for giving bite and texture, walnuts have a very distinctive taste, but you could use either hazelnuts, almonds or a mixture of different nuts. This cake will also keep well for up to 7 days if it is wrapped in greaseproof paper and kept in an airtight tin or container.

PREPARATION TIME: about 10 minutes
COOKING TIME: see chart
OVEN: 180°C, 350°F, Gas mark 4

1 Grease all the bakeware you will require with a little melted butter or margarine, then line the base with greaseproof paper and grease again.

2 Put the grated carrot and apple, chopped nuts of your choice, vegetable oil, soft brown sugar, honey and eggs into a bowl and mix thoroughly using a wooden spoon.

ℋEALTHY SPONGE CAKE

★ FOOTBALL ★ MOUSE PICNIC ★ PINK PIGGY ★ THREE-TIER TEDDY ★

	18 CM (7 INCH) ROUND TIN	1.2 LITRE (2 PINT) BOWL	20 CM (8 INCH) SQUARE TIN	12 CM (5 INCH) ROUND TIN AND 7 CM (3 INCH) DIAMETER MUG
SIZE	1	2	3	4
carrot, grated	175g (6oz)	175g (6oz)	175g (6oz)	125g (4oz)
apple, grated	175g (6oz)	175g (6oz)	175g (6oz)	125g (4oz)
nuts, chopped	75g (3oz)	75g (3oz)	75g (3oz)	50g (2oz)
vegetable oil	125ml (4fl oz)	125ml (4fl oz)	125ml (4fl oz)	100ml (3½fl oz)
soft brown sugar	125g (4oz)	125g (4oz)	125g (4oz)	75g (3oz)
clear honey	2 tablespoons	2 tablespoons	2 tablespoons	1½ tablespoons
eggs (size 3)	2	1	2	1
egg yolk	–	1	–	1
plain flour	125g (4oz)	125g (4oz)	125g (4oz)	75g (3oz)
wholemeal plain flour	125g (4oz)	125g (4oz)	125g (4oz)	75g (3oz)
bicarbonate of soda	1 teaspoon	1 teaspoon	1 teaspoon	¾ teaspoon
ground cinnamon	2 teaspoons	2 teaspoons	2 teaspoons	1½ teaspoons
salt	pinch	pinch	pinch	pinch
cooking time	1-1¼ hours	1-1¼ hours	40 minutes	1-1¼ hours (large cake) 25-30 minutes (small cake)

3 Sift together the plain and wholemeal flour, bicarbonate of soda, cinnamon and salt. Stir into the carrot mixture until thoroughly and evenly blended.

4 Turn into the ready prepared bakeware and level the top with a slightly wetted metal spoon. Bake in a preheated oven for the time suggested in the chart or until it is well risen and nicely firm to the touch.

5 Allow to cool in the bakeware for about 10 minutes, then turn it out onto a wire rack. Leave the cake to cool for at least 8 hours before using to cut and shape.

Variations: To make this cake a little different, according to your own particular taste, you can adapt the ingredients of this cake in many ways. For instance, replace 25g (1oz) of the chopped nuts with 25g (1oz) of chopped fresh or dried dates or 25g (1oz) chopped ready-to-eat dried apricots or pears. Replace the clear honey with a scented variety such as orange blossom or lime blossom. If it is too thick, heat it in a small saucepan over a very gentle heat until it is a little more runny. Finally, replace the ground cinnamon with any combination of spices you like, such as nutmeg, ginger or even cloves.

Below: Healthy sponge cake

LIGHT FRUIT CAKE

This well-flavoured cake keeps for about 2 weeks in an airtight container.

PREPARATION TIME: about 20 minutes
COOKING TIME: see chart
OVEN: 180°C, 350°F, Gas mark 4

1 Grease the bakeware, line the base with a double layer of greaseproof paper and grease again.

2 Sift the flour, bicarbonate of soda, spice and ginger into a bowl.

3 In another bowl, cream the butter and sugar until light, fluffy and pale.

4 Beat in the eggs, one at a time, following each with a spoonful of the flour mixture, then very gently fold in the remaining flour.

5 Add the raisins, currants, sultanas, mixed peel, fruit rind and apple to the mixture and stir until evenly blended.

6 Turn into the prepared bakeware and level the top. Bake in the centre of a preheated oven for the time suggested in the chart.

7 The cake is done when a skewer inserted into the centre comes out clean. Cool in the bakeware, then turn out on to a rack and leave until cold. Do not peel off the lining paper, but wrap in foil and store in an airtight container for 24-48 hours before cutting.

Right: Light fruit cake

*L*IGHT FRUIT CAKE

★ FOOTBALL ★ HUMPTY DUMPTY ★ PINK PIGGY ★

	18 CM (7 INCH) SQUARE TIN	1.2 LITRE (2 PINT) BOWL	8 CM (3½ INCH) DIAMETER BOWL AND 8CM (3½ INCH) DIAMETER MUG
SIZE	1	2	3
plain flour	225g (8oz)	175g (6oz)	50g (2oz)
bicarbonate of soda	½ teaspoon	⅓ teaspoon	good pinch
mixed spice	½ teaspoon	⅓ teaspoon	good pinch
ground ginger	¼ teaspoon	good pinch	pinch
butter or margarine	175g (6oz)	125g (4oz)	40g (1½oz)
light soft brown sugar	175g (6oz)	125g (4oz)	40g (1½oz)
eggs	2 (sizes 1 or 2)	2 (sizes 3 or 4)	1 (size 5)
raisins	225g (8oz)	175g (6oz)	50g (2oz)
currants	125g (4oz)	75g (3oz)	25g (1oz)
sultanas	125g (4oz)	75g (3oz)	25g (1oz)
cut mixed peel	50g (2oz)	40g (1½oz)	15g (½oz)
grated orange or lemon rind	1 orange or lemon	1 orange or lemon	½ orange or lemon
apple, grated	175g (6oz)	125g (4oz)	25g (1oz)
cooking time	1¼-1½ hours	1-1¼ hours	30 minutes

RICH FRUIT CAKE

This fruit cake recipe was given to me by my mother who has honed it to perfection after many years of baking. It really does make a sumptuously, delicious, dark and moist cake which is perfect for any kind of celebration, but it is perhaps particularly appropriate for the Christmas season and festivities. Although the cake is at its best 3 months after baking, eating it before or after this time doesn't matter. Keep wrapped until you are ready to eat it.

PREPARATION TIME: 30 minutes
COOKING TIME: see chart
OVEN: 150°C, 300°F, Gas mark 2

1 Grease the cake tin, line with a double layer of greaseproof paper and grease again.

2 Quarter, wash and thoroughly dry the glacé cherries and then place in a large clean bowl.

3 Add the sultanas, currants, raisins, mixed peel, ground almonds, chopped nuts, grated lemon rind and mixed spice. Mix well.

4 In another bowl, cream the butter and sugar until light, fluffy and pale.

5 Beat the eggs into the creamed mixture, one at a time, following each with a spoonful of the flour.

6 Add the black treacle.

7 Fold in the remaining flour and add the dried fruit mixture.

8 Turn the mixture into the prepared tin and level the top, then make a dip in the centre with the back of a spoon.

9 Tie a double layer of brown paper round the outside of the tin to protect the cake during cooking and place on a baking sheet lined with a double layer of brown paper.

10 Bake for the suggested cooking time and test by inserting a skewer into the centre. If it comes out clean the cake is done. If not, put it back into the oven for about 10 minutes more and then check again.

11 Leave the cake to cool in the tin. When cold, remove from the tin and wrap in greaseproof paper, then in foil. A final wrap of clingfilm will help keep the cake moist during storage.

12 To improve flavour and lengthen keeping time, pierce the top of the cake with a skewer and spoon several tablespoons of brandy or other spirit over it.

Variation: If you would like to make this cake a little lighter in colour, replace the black treacle with 1 tablespoon of golden syrup and replace the soft brown sugar with 225g (8oz) caster sugar.

*R*ICH FRUIT CAKE

★ CHRISTMAS TOY CHEST ★

	20 CM (8 INCH) SQUARE TIN
glacé cherries	125g (4oz)
sultanas	350g (12oz)
currants	225g (8oz)
raisins	125g (4oz)
cut mixed peel	50g (2oz)
ground almonds	50g (2oz)
mixed chopped nuts	50g (2oz)
grated lemon rind	I lemon
mixed spice	I teaspoon
butter	225g (8oz)
soft brown sugar	225g (8oz)
eggs (size 2)	4
plain flour	250g (9oz)
black treacle	I tablespoon
cooking time	3³/₄ hours

Right: Rich fruit cake

Icings and Fillings

The following recipes include all the icings and fillings you will need throughout the book. For instructions on how to colour icing, see page 23.

FONDANT ICING

Fondant icing (sugarpaste) can be bought from cake decorating suppliers, supermarkets and other outlets. Some brands are easier to use than others, so it is best to try a few to find the one you work with best. The ready-made icing is usually of high quality, but if you prefer to make your own, here is the recipe. As a general rule, this icing is rolled to a thickness of 3 mm (¹/₈ inch) before use.

MAKES 675g (1¹/₂lb)
1 egg white
2 tablespoons liquid glucose
675g (1¹/₂lb) icing sugar, sifted
a little white fat (optional)

1 Put the egg white and liquid glucose into a bowl and gradually add the icing sugar. Stir until the mixture thickens.

2 Turn out on to a surface dusted with icing sugar and knead until the paste is smooth and silky. If the paste becomes a little dry and cracked, try kneading in a little white fat.

MODELLING FONDANT

This is fondant icing with gum tragacanth added. It makes the icing firmer and easy to shape into figures, animals and small objects but, once unwrapped, you have to work extremely quickly as it starts to dry after only a few minutes.

Below: Gelatine icing

Gum tragacanth is available in powder form from cake decorating suppliers and some chemists.

MAKES 450g (1lb)
2 teaspoons gum tragacanth
450g (1lb) fondant icing

1 Put the gum tragacanth on a clean surface and knead into the fondant. Wrap in a polythene bag and leave for about 8 hours before use to allow the gum to take effect.

GELATINE ICING

This icing dries very hard, very quickly. It is suitable for making free-standing sugar items as it will not bend or lose shape when completely dry. It can be used as a modelling fondant, but as it crusts so quickly I recommend you mix it with fondant icing in equal amounts.

MAKES 725g (1lb 10oz)
3 tablespoons water
2 heaped teaspoons powdered gelatine
1 tablespoon liquid glucose
1 egg white
725g (1lb 10oz) icing sugar, sifted

1 Put the water in a bowl and sprinkle on the gelatine powder. Leave for a few moments then place the bowl over a pan of hot water. As soon as the gelatine has dissolved completely, gently stir in the liquid glucose, then follow with the egg white. Add about three-quarters of the sifted icing sugar, a little at a time, and stir with a wooden spoon until the mixture thickens.

2 Turn out on to a surface liberally dusted with icing sugar and knead thoroughly, incorporating the remaining icing sugar.

3 Wrap the icing in a polythene bag and store in an airtight container for up to 2 weeks.

Left: Royal icing which throughout the book is useful for piping and styling hair and sticking modelled items together.

Below: Figures made from modelling fondant

ROYAL ICING

When I first started cake decorating I was terrified of piping with royal icing and avoided it as long as I could, but once I started, I realized just how simple it really is. With a little practice, you will too. It is difficult to make up smaller quantities than the recipe given, but it can be stored in an airtight container in a cool place, such as a refrigerator, for approximately 10 days. It must be stirred thoroughly before use.

See page 25 to find out how to fold a paper piping bag.

MAKES ABOUT 225g (8oz)
1 egg white
1 teaspoon lemon juice
225-250g (8-9oz) icing sugar, sifted

1 Put the egg white and lemon juice into a bowl and beat in the icing sugar, a little at a time, until the icing is smooth, white, and forms soft peaks when the spoon is pulled out.

2 Cover the bowl with a damp cloth and leave to stand for 5 minutes to disperse any air bubbles before use. Store in an airtight container in the refrigerator for up to 10 days.

MARZIPAN

Ready-made marzipan or almond paste is widely available from most major supermarkets, especially at Christmas, but if you make your own you can vary the colour. For a white marzipan, replace the egg with 2 egg whites; for a brighter yellow version, use 2 egg yolks. As marzipan does not freeze well, it is best to make up only the required quantity.

MAKES 450g (1lb)
125g (4oz) icing sugar, sifted
125g (4oz) caster sugar
225g (8oz) ground almonds
1 egg, lightly beaten
1 teaspoon lemon juice
few drops of almond essence

1 Put the sugars and almonds into a bowl. Add the egg, lemon juice and almond essence and mix together until it forms a stiff dough.

2 Turn out on to a surface dusted with icing sugar and knead until smooth. Wrap in a polythene bag and store for 2-3 days.

APRICOT GLAZE

This is best made shortly before you need it. It can be made up to a week ahead and stored in an airtight container in the refrigerator, but it will have to be boiled and cooled again before using.

MAKES 150ml (¼ pint)
150g (5oz) apricot jam
2-3 tablespoons water

1 Put the jam and water into a saucepan and heat gently, stirring occasionally, until the jam melts. Simmer gently for 1-2 minutes.

2 Rub through a sieve and allow to cool slightly before using.

Variations: Apricot jam is probably the most versatile jam to use for making a glaze, which forms a layer between the surface of the cake and the icing, because it is a fairly neutral colour. However, you could just as easily use the same quantities of raspberry jam and water to make a raspberry glaze. This should only be used on cakes where the icing is dark as it can show through the pale colours. Another alternative is to use redcurrant jelly. As this is a fairly soft jelly, be careful to use only a small quantity of water otherwise it may not be so sticky once it has been brushed on to the cake.

Left: Apricot glaze; Marzipan

BUTTER CREAM

Butter cream is easy to work with and has many uses when making novelty cakes.

MAKES 350g (12oz)
125g (4oz) butter or soft margarine
225g (8oz) icing sugar, sifted
few drops of vanilla flavouring
1-2 tablespoons milk or water

1 Put the butter in a bowl and cream until very soft.

2 Gradually beat in the icing sugar, adding vanilla to taste, and just enough milk or water to give a firm but spread-able consistency. If not using straight-away, store in an airtight container in the refrigerator for up to 1 week. Allow to return to room temperature before using.

VARIATION: Chocolate Butter Cream
Dissolve 1-2 tablespoons sifted cocoa powder in a little hot water to give a thin paste. Allow to cool slightly before beating into the butter cream in place of the milk.

CONTINENTAL BUTTER CREAM

A deliciously rich, smooth butter cream for sandwiching cakes together.

MAKES ABOUT 275g (10oz)
75g (3oz) caster sugar
4 tablespoons water
2 egg yolks
175g (6oz) unsalted butter

1 Put the sugar and water into a small, heavy-based saucepan and heat gen-tly until the sugar dissolves completely.

2 Put a sugar thermometer into the pan, bring up to the boil, and then boil steadily for 2-3 minutes, until the syrup reaches 110°C, 225°F. If you do not have a sugar thermometer, try the thread test: dip the back of a teaspoon into the syrup and pull the syrup away with the back of another spoon. It should form a thin thread. If this does not happen, boil for another minute and test again.

3 Put the egg yolks into a large bowl and whisk well (a hand-held electric mixer is best, but a balloon or rotary whisk will do). Whisking constantly, pour the syrup in a thin stream on to the yolks (not on to the mixer or bowl). Continue whisking until the mixture is thick and cool.

4 In another bowl, cream the butter until soft and light, then beat in the egg yolk mixture a little at a time, until smooth and spreadable.

Above left: Continental butter cream; above right: butter cream

Equipment and Techniques

The following information outlines equipment and techniques that are useful to both the beginner and practised cake maker.

There are hundreds of items you can buy to help with cake decorating, but if you are not an avid cake maker and decorator and only make cakes when the need arises, there are plenty of items from your kitchen cupboards that you can use instead of going out and breaking the bank!

For baking the cakes, different containers such as ovenproof bowls and mugs can be put to excellent use. For any circles that need to be cut, instead of using special plain circle cutters, as a guide to cut around you can use cups, mugs and egg-cups of the required size.

For decorating cakes, a sharp knife, a rolling pin and a few cocktail sticks are essential, but the rest you can improvise with items from your kitchen.

Cake boards

Cake boards come in a variety of shapes and sizes and are usually covered in silver foil, although gold and metallic red are obtainable. To make your cake look even better, I recommend you cover the board with fondant icing. Alternatively you can use colour co-ordinating paper, as long as it is greaseproof. Glue the paper to the cake board with a mixture of 2 teaspoons flour mixed to a paste with a few drops of water. Brush thinly on to the surface of the board using a pastry brush, cover with the paper, then leave to dry.

Greaseproof paper piping bags

These can be purchased ready cut to shape in small and large sizes, but a triangular shape cut from a sheet of greaseproof paper or baking parchment will fold just as well (see page 25).

Piping nozzles

I recommend that you use good quality piping nozzles, which, although more expensive, do last a lifetime. The basic writing nozzles in sizes 1–4 are used in this book for piping royal icing and indenting shapes using both ends.

Small rolling pin

This is useful for rolling out small pieces of fondant icing as a large rolling pin can be quite clumsy.

Turntable

For easy access to all sides of the cake you are working on, I recommend that

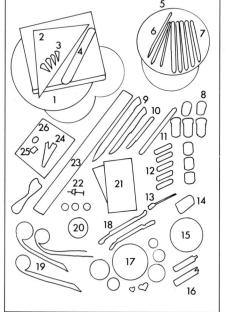

The following list is a guide to some of the useful items available from cake decorating suppliers (see page 86).

1 Cake boards
2 Greaseproof piping bags
3 Piping nozzles
4 Small rolling pin
5 Turntable
6 Paintbrushes
7 Food colouring pens
8 Food colouring pastes
9 Knives
10 Craft knife
11 Wooden and plastic skewers (dowelling)
12 Powder colours
13 Miniature brush
14 Gum arabic
15 Garrett frill cutter
16 Crimping tools
17 Basic cutters
18 Modelling tools
19 Ribbons
20 Pins
21 Smoother with handle
22 Plunger and blossom cutters
23 Ruler
24 Cocktail sticks
25 Embossing stamps
26 Foam

you use a turntable. The one shown here is metal, which can be quite expensive, but cheaper plastic ones are obtainable. If you prefer, an upturned tin could be used.

Paintbrushes
I recommend that you use good quality sable paintbrushes as they do not shed hairs like the cheaper versions. The basic sizes shown here should be enough to start.

Food colouring pens
These are felt tip pens filled with food colouring and come in a rainbow of colours and are extremely useful. Always use them after the icing has dried as the colour can spread.

Food colouring pastes
These come in a vast range of colours, but the basic primaries, red, blue, yellow and black are all you need to start with as you can mix these to achieve different colours.

Knives
To help with your cake decorating, make sure you have good sharp knives to work with in a variety of sizes.

Craft knife
Very useful for cutting out small pieces of fondant. Replacement blades can be purchased.

Wooden and plastic skewers (dowelling)
These are used to help support the cakes that stand quite high. I have also used them for the Wicked Witch's broom handle (see page 74) and the golf clubs in the Golf Bag cake (see page 40).

Powder colours
These come in a variety of colours, plain or lustre. Brushed on with a dry paintbrush, they give just a hint of colour or sparkle, but can be quite messy to use. You can also mix them

to a paste with a few drops of clear alcohol or water for painting on dry icing, which is especially effective with the silver and gold lustre powders.

Miniature brush
Very helpful in brushing away any loose icing sugar left on the cake and as it is so small, it will get to any awkward corner.

Gum arabic
Available from any cake decorating supplier, this white powder is used as a glue to stick items on to cakes. Mix together a small amount with a few drops of water.

Garrett frill cutter
This garrett frill cutter has a removable inner circle so you can use other circle cutters to change the depth of the frill (see page 24 on how to make a garrett frill).

Crimping tools
These are available in many shapes and are used to make patterns by gently pinching the fondant icing together. It is often used to create a decorative border on the fondant icing covered cake board.

Basic cutters
There are many special cutters which are available in different sizes and designs. A basic set of plastic or metal circle cutters are especially useful.

Modelling tools
These can work out to be expensive items. However, children's plastic craft tools available from toy and craft shops work out much cheaper and do the job just as well.

Ribbons
Using ribbons with co-ordinating colours and patterns for the cake board banding, adds the finishing flourish to your cake. Remember, if you are going to ice the board, you will need a slightly

wider ribbon than if you do not. Use a pin to hold the ribbon in place at the back of the board. If you don't want the pin to show, you can disguise it with a small ribbon bow.

Pins
Pins are used to hold the ribbon banding in place on the cake board. They can also be used to make small marks or patterns on the icing.

Smoother with handle
This is used for smoothing out any dents in the icing to get a good finish. To use the smoother see page 24.

Plunger and blossom cutters
These blossom cutters attach to the end of the plunger and when used, make a prettily-shaped flower with an indented centre. When making the blossoms always push out on to a piece of foam as this helps to give shape to the flower and they also dry more quickly. Different shapes can be bought to attach to the plunger, such as a bow shape.

Ruler
Used for any accurate measuring required, but also for any straight line you wish to mark into the fondant icing.

Cocktail sticks
These are used to add colour to the icing (see page 23), and they have no end of uses when making modelled items or marking details on a cake.

Embossing stamps
These are designs with a raised outline, which when pushed gently into fondant icing, make an impression.

Foam
Your modelling work dries much quicker if placed on a piece of foam, as the air can circulate underneath as well as above. Foam is also used when making plunger flowers, as the centre of each flower is pressed into the foam to give it more shape.

COLOURING METHODS

I recommend you use the paste or concentrated liquid food colouring obtainable from cake decorating suppliers. The liquid form sold in most supermarkets can make your icing too wet, especially if you have to achieve a deep colour. However, it is fine if only a pale shade is required.

Powdered food colouring can be quite messy, so it is best to use it only for dusting on when the icing is dry to achieve just a hint of colour. Edible gold and silver powder can be painted on to the icing after mixing with a few drops of clear alcohol, such as vodka or gin, or just plain water.

Food colouring pens come in many shades and avoid the need for paintbrushes. Only use the pens on icing that has had at least a day to dry out and before you start, brush off any excess icing sugar from the surface to prevent the food colouring from spreading out. If you have difficulty obtaining these pens, you can paint on the dry icing using concentrated food colouring that has been watered down to a watercolour paint consistency. Again, thoroughly brush off any loose icing sugar to prevent the colour from spreading.

How to colour fondant
Put a little colour on the end of a cocktail stick and add to the fondant. Fold it in and knead thoroughly until the colour is even throughout, with no streaks. If you require a deep colour, keep adding more food colouring a little at a time until you achieve the shade you want.

How to colour royal icing
Put a little colour on the end of a cocktail stick, add to the royal icing and stir well. You will find that this icing takes colour very easily and bright colours such as red and yellow can get brighter, so leave the royal icing covered with a damp cloth for a few minutes for the colours to develop.

How to roll out fondant
Take the required amount of fondant and knead it a little to warm it up. Dust the surface liberally with icing sugar to prevent the paste from sticking. Press the fondant on to the icing sugar, turn over and press again, then roll out the fondant, moving it around frequently

Above: Royal icing in a rainbow of pastel colours

so that it doesn't stick to the surface. Continue rolling out until it is about 3 mm (¹/₈ inch) thick.

Helpful Hints

The following tips are intended to give helpful advice and practical information to instructions that arise throughout this book.

How to smooth a cake surface

Cake smoothers are invaluable, as your hands alone will not get a perfect surface. They are relatively cheap and are available from cake decorating suppliers. The cake smoother with a handle is best for novelty cakes as it has rounded edges. Rub the surface of the cake in a circular motion, pressing quite firmly to remove any dents in the fondant.

Joins in the fondant should be removed before the icing starts to dry by rubbing with your fingers in a circular motion.

How to stick pieces of fondant together

A little water applied with a fine paintbrush will stick fondant icing together, but it is not strong enough for large pieces or for your modelling fondant figures. I recommend you use a little egg white or, if you prefer, gum arabic, which is an edible glue available in powder form from cake decorating suppliers.

How to make a garrett frill

Garrett frill cutters are available from cake decorating suppliers. Alternatively you can use a fluted cutter and a smaller plain cutter to achieve the same effect. Roll out a small amount of fondant quite thinly and cut with the garrett frill cutter or fluted and plain cutters. Using a cocktail stick dipped in cornflour, roll the end of the stick over each loop gently until the icing becomes thin and starts to frill. Work round until the circle is completely

frilled, then cut open. Dampen the surface of the cake with a little water to stick the garrett frill in place, see Lazy Days page 29.

How to mix colouring pastes and gold and silver lustre powders for painting

Clear alcohol should be used in preference to water, as it evaporates more quickly. For the colouring pastes, place a quantity of alcohol into a small bowl and using a cocktail stick dip it into the paste and add to the alcohol. Keep adding a little at a time until the desired colour is achieved. For the gold and silver lustre powders, mix 1 teaspoon of clear alcohol with $1/2$–1 teaspoon of powder to make a soft paste.

How to cover a cake board with fondant icing

Roll out the fondant icing. Dampen the cake board with a little water, then place the icing on the board and smooth with a cake smoother to get a completely flat surface. Trim the edges with a sharp knife.

How to cover a cake board with green coconut

Place 6–8 tablespoons of desiccated coconut into a polythene bag with some green food colouring. Hold the bag closed and rub the colour into the coconut.

Spread the cake board with 125–175g (4–6oz) of green-coloured royal icing, then sprinkle on the green coconut.

Leave to dry for at least 2 hours.

How to grease and line a baking tin or ovenproof bowl

Place the cake tin on to a sheet of clean greaseproof paper and mark the outline with a pencil. Cut around the outline using a pair of sharp scissors. To measure the sides of the tin, take a piece of string and wrap it round the outside, use this to cut out another piece of greaseproof paper. Melt a little butter or margarine in a saucepan, then brush a thin coat on to the inside of the tin. Position both the cut-out base and sides inside the tin. Brush another thin layer of grease over the paper.

If you need to line an ovenproof bowl, cut a small circle out of greaseproof paper, large enough to cover the base only. Brush the inside of the bowl with melted fat, then position the cut-out paper in the bottom of the bowl.

How to make blossom flowers

The easiest way to make small blossom flowers is to use a blossom plunger cutter. The blossom cutters come in varying sizes and each attach to the end of a plunger. Push the end of the plunger cutter into the rolled out fondant icing to cut out a flower. Gently wipe the edges of the flower cutter with your thumb to remove any loose particles, then rest the plunger cutter on a piece of foam. Holding the plunger like an injection needle, push out the fondant flower into the foam to indent the centre. If you don't want to pipe a centre with royal icing, push the tip of a plain piping nozzle in the middle of the flower to mark the centre.

HOW TO MAKE A GREASEPROOF PAPER PIPING BAG

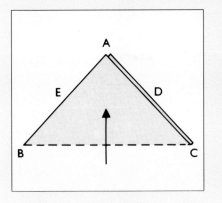

1 Cut a 25 cm (10 inch) square and fold to form a triangle.

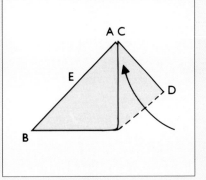

2 Fold point C across to point A and crease firmly.

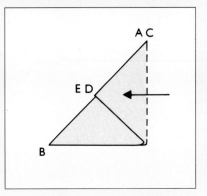

3 Fold point D and point E and again, crease firmly.

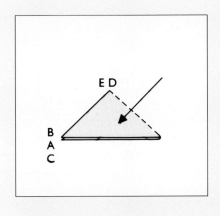

4 Fold point AC down to point B and crease firmly. Holding the bag at ED, open it out to make a cone.

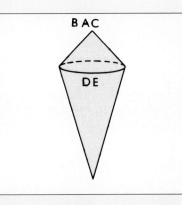

5 Secure the join well with some adhesive tape and fold the top part down firmly inside the cone.

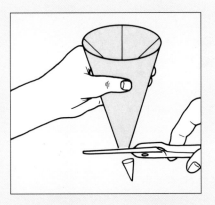

6 Cut off the tip of the paper bag so that the nozzle will fit neatly with about one-third of it showing.

FACTS AND FIGURES

- Unless otherwise stated, all spoon measurements given in this book are level and all eggs are size 2.

- Both metric and imperial measurements have been calculated separately. Use one set of measurements only as they are not exact equivalents. In some recipes, you may find an apparent discrepancy in the metric equivalent. This is done to ensure a correct proportion of ingredients.

- Cooking times may vary slightly depending on the individual oven. Cakes should be placed in the centre of the oven unless otherwise specified. Always preheat the oven to the specified temperature.

- All icing is assumed to be coloured before you start following the recipe and all basic cakes baked. For detailed instructions on how to colour all kinds of icing see page 23.

- All icing used should be rolled to a thickness of 3 mm (⅛ inch) unless otherwise stated.

- All skewers in the text refer to plastic or wooden dowelling that can be bought from hardware stores and specialist cake decorating suppliers.

Laughing Clown

This lively and colourful clown will perform his juggling tricks and brighten up any party.

You WILL NEED:

5 Madeira cakes (size 3, size 4, size 5, size 6)
1.9kg (4lb 3oz) fondant icing
red, yellow, blue, flesh, orange and black food colouring paste
450g (1lb) butter cream
egg white or gum arabic

EQUIPMENT:

7-8 cocktail sticks
25 cm (10 inch) round cake board
10 cm (4 inch) plain circle cutter
skewer
fine paintbrush
piping nozzle or mini circle cutter
garrett frill cutter
large flower cutter

COLOUR:

Fondant icing:
300g (11oz) red, 450g (1lb) yellow, 450g (1lb) blue, 225g (8oz) flesh, 300g (11oz) orange, 125g (4oz) white, 25g (1oz) black

1 Cover the cake board with 275g (10oz) of the red fondant and leave to dry. Reserve the trimmings.

2 Slice the tops off all the cakes so they are completely flat, then cut the mug cake in half to make 2 circles.

3 Place the large bowl cake on top of the 15 cm (6 inch) round cake. To mark the arms, make a cut about 1 cm (½ inch) deep, and continue to cut in a curving line down to the bottom of the bowl cake. Mark the back of the arm with a similar curving line 5 cm (2 inches) behind the first line. Repeat for the other arm.

4 Slice the front flat down to the bottom of the bowl cake and trim round to the arms. Repeat for the back of the cake, trimming any sharp angles.

5 Keeping the width at the top of the 15 cm (6 inch) round cake, trim the base by about 5 mm (¼ inch) all the way round, cutting at an inwards angle. Cut a small triangle out of the front and the back to mark the trouser legs.

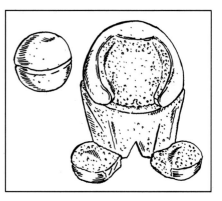

6 To make the shoes, trim the tops of the 2 circle cakes so they slope down on one side, then trim the sides to make oval shapes. Cut the ends so they fit against the bottom of the trousers.

7 To give the clown a little more height, cut a layer in the 15 cm (6 inch) round cake and spread 125g (4oz) of the butter cream in the layer. Spread another 125g (4oz) between the 2 cakes to stick them together, then spread a thin layer of butter cream all over the cake. Place the cake on the cake board.

8 Sandwich the 2 small bowl cakes together with butter cream to make the head, and trim the front flat for the face. Spread a thin layer of butter cream all over the head and set aside.

9 Roll out 150g (5oz) of the yellow fondant and cut in half. Cover each shoe and indent the tops with the 10 cm (4 inch) circle cutter. Roll out the remaining yellow fondant and cover the top of the cake, trimming at the top of the 15 cm (6 inch) round cake. Mark the arm creases with a knife.

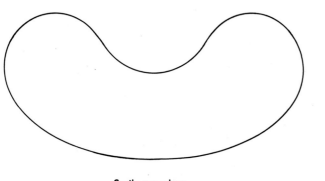

Smile template

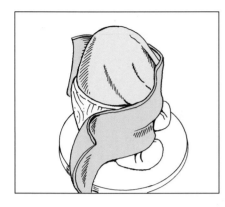

19 To make the juggling balls, roll the leftover yellow and red fondant into 2 equal-sized balls. Cut each ball into quarters and stick 4 alternate coloured quarters together with a little egg white or gum arabic. Make 2 red and yellow balls. Leave the cake to dry for at least 8 hours, or overnight.

10 To make the trousers, roll out 300g (11oz) of the blue fondant into an oblong measuring 10 x 50 cm (4 x 20 inches). Wrap round the base of the cake, making the join at the back. Fold the top inwards for the waistband and mark between the legs with a knife.

11 Roll out the flesh-coloured fondant to cover the head, tucking the fondant underneath and making the join at the back – don't worry if the back looks untidy, as it will be covered with hair later. Place the head on the cake and push the skewer down through the top of the head to keep it in place.

little egg white or gum arabic. Roll the remaining white fondant into 2 balls and shape into the hands, making 4 cuts for the fingers. Cut 2 strips of blue fondant for the braces and stick both the hands and braces in place with the thumbs tucked under.

14 With the red fondant trimmings, model the clown's nose and 4 red buttons for the braces. Cut 15-20 circles with the end of a piping nozzle or mini circle cutter and stick on the clown's top. Make 2 garrett frills (see page 24) and cut one in half. Place one round the clown's neck and the 2 halves round the sleeves.

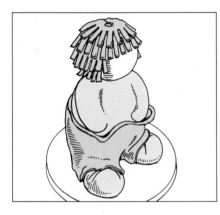

12 Roll out the orange fondant thickly and cut into five 4 cm (1½ inch) wide strips. Make cuts almost to the top of the strips, 5 mm (¼ inch) apart, then stick on to the clown's head with a little egg white or gum arabic, starting from the bottom and overlapping each layer.

13 With 25g (1oz) of the white fondant, roll out and cut a smile, see template, and 2 eyes, then stick in place with a

15 Make a ball with 65g (2½oz) of the blue fondant, then roll out another 65g (2½oz) and place it over the ball. Smooth round, then place the 10 cm (4 inch) circle cutter over the top to cut a hat. Place the hat on the head and lift the rim slightly to flute.

16 Roll out the red fondant trimmings and cut out the smile, and a strip for the hat ribbon; stick in place with a little egg white or gum arabic. Model a flower centre.

17 Roll out the yellow fondant trimmings and cut out a flower with the flower cutter; stick in place on top of the hat, adding in the red centre.

18 Cut 4 thin strips of black fondant and stick on the eyes with a little egg white or gum arabic.

Alternative design:

Instead of making the juggling balls to accompany the clown, try making juggling clubs. Use the same yellow and red fondant trimmings, but just mould into club shapes. You should be able to make about 3 or 4 clubs. Place them at the feet of the clown.

Lazy Days

This cake is a good idea for a retirement celebration, or perhaps a hint to your other half that he watches too much television with his feet up.

You will need:

1 Madeira cake (size 2)
1.55kg (3lb 7oz) fondant icing
450g (1lb) modelling fondant
2 teaspoons royal icing
peach, egg yellow, black, blue, flesh
  and brown food colouring paste
900g (2lb) butter cream
green, blue and black food
  colouring pens
egg white or gum arabic

Equipment:

7-8 cocktail sticks
35 cm (14 inch) round cake board
crimping tool
No. 3 piping nozzle
7 cm (3 inch) plain circle cutter
star tool
garrett frill cutter
fine paintbrush

Colour:

Fondant icing: 450g (1lb) peach,
  1.1kg (2lb 7oz) cream (a touch of
  egg yellow)
Modelling fondant: 150g (5oz) grey,
  75g (3oz) blue, 125g (4oz) white,
  50g (2oz) flesh, 50g (2oz) brown
Royal icing: 2 teaspoons coloured
  grey (a touch of black)

1 Cover the cake board with 375g (13oz) of the peach fondant icing and cut a frill all round the edge with a knife. Crimp a line above the frill, using the crimping tool. Set aside and leave to dry.

2 Slice the top off the cake so it is completely flat.

3 Cut the cake as shown so you have the base of the chair measuring 12 x 12 cm (5 x 5 inches), the chair back measuring 7 x 12 cm (3 x 5 inches) and the chair arms measuring 4 x 10 cm (1½ x 4 inches) each. The 2 tables are cut next, using the 7 cm (3 inch) circle cutter, and the footstool measures 6 x 8 cm (2½ x 3½ inches). With the remaining cake, cut a cushion for the chair base measuring 5 x 7 cm (2 x 3 inches), and 2 cm (¾ inch) in depth.

4 Cut a layer in each of the table cakes and spread with butter cream to give a little more height. Spread a thin layer of butter cream all over both table cakes and the footstool.

5 Trim the end of the arms so that they fit the chair, then trim the tops to round them off.

6 Cut 2 small 'V' shapes out of the top and front part of the chair back, as shown above, 3 cm (1½ inches) in from either side, then round off and neaten the edges. This adds extra detail.

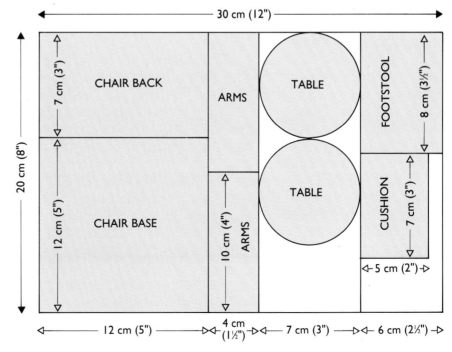

7 Spread half of the remaining butter cream on top of the chair base to stick the chair back, cushion and arms in place. Spread a thin layer of butter cream all over the chair cake.

8 Roll out 200g (7oz) of the cream-coloured fondant icing, then lay the back of the chair on to it and cut round. To cover the rest of the chair, roll out 450g (1lb) of fondant and lay it over the front, top and sides, smoothing down to shape. Trim, then smooth out the joins by rubbing with your fingers in a circular motion. Using the end of a piping nozzle and a cocktail stick, mark the detail on the chair arm and front.

9 Roll out 50g (2oz) of the cream-coloured fondant to 3 mm ($^1/_8$ inch) thick, then place the top of the footstool down on to it and cut round. This helps to pad out the footstool. Roll out 75g (3oz) and cover the footstool completely. With a star tool, indent the top of the footstool 4 times.

10 Place the chair cake on the cake board. Make the garrett frills from cream-coloured fondant (see page 24), and stick round the base of the chair and footstool. Mark a line above the frill using the crimping tool. Place the footstool on the cake board.

11 Roll out 2 pieces of cream-coloured fondant, 150g (5oz) each, and cut 2 circles measuring 18 cm (7 inch) in diameter. Place one over each table cake, encouraging the pleats for the tablecloth, then position on the cake board, pushing the lamp table right up against the chair. Roll 25g (1oz) of the fondant into a ball for the lamp base. Stick in place with a little egg white or gum arabic.

12 Divide the remaining peach fondant into 3 pieces, and model 2 cushions and the lampshade, marking the lines with a cocktail stick. Stick in place.

13 With 75g (3oz) of the grey modelling fondant, model the television, then mark the outline of the screen and the speaker lines with a knife. Push in the tip of the No. 3 piping nozzle to mark the buttons. Use the remaining grey modelling fondant to make the 2 slippers and the TV remote control, then set aside to dry. Colour a small amount a slightly darker grey and roll out. Cut a television screen to fit and stick in place with a little egg white or gum arabic.

14 Roll the blue modelling fondant into a long sausage shape and cut down the centre to make the legs, leaving 2.5 cm (1 inch) for the top of the trousers. Stick on the chair with a little egg white or gum arabic, crossing over the legs and resting them on the footstool.

15 To model the jumper, take 75g (3oz) of the white modelling fondant and roll into a ball. Flatten slightly, then cut the 2 arms. Hollow the bottom a little by pushing in your thumb, then stick in position, as shown above.

16 Using 25g (1oz) of the flesh-coloured modelling fondant, roll a ball for the head. With the remaining 25g (1oz), model 2 feet and stick in place, then model 2 hands and set aside.

17 With the remaining white modelling fondant, make the newspapers, the cup and saucer and the book's pages. Roll out the peach fondant trimmings

and wrap round the book. Stick the hands in place, one holding a newspaper and the other holding the remote control.

18 Cut the brown modelling fondant in half and use one half to model the dog's body. With the other half, model the dog's head, nose, ears, 2 paws and a tail. With the cream fondant trimmings, model a circle for the dog collar. Stick all the pieces together using a little egg white or gum arabic, then place on the cake board. Put a tiny ball of brown fondant into the cup, gently pushing it down with the end of a paintbrush.

19 Spread the grey royal icing on to the man's head and 'curl' with a cocktail stick. Put some royal icing on the end of the cocktail stick and draw the eyebrows. Leave the cake to dry for at least 8 hours, or overnight.

20 Mix a tiny amount of peach food colouring paste with a few drops of water and, using the paintbrush, paint the roses on the chair and footstool. Paint small dots on the tablecloths.

21 With the green food colouring pen, draw the leaf design on the chair and the footstool and with the blue food colouring pen, decorate the cup. With the green and blue pens, draw the tartan design on the slippers. With the black pen, draw the eyes and all the writing on the newspapers.

Right: Lazy days

Three-Tier Teddy

A bright and pretty cake that is easy to decorate. To make it even easier, you could buy the animals and flowers ready made.

You will need:

3 healthy sponge cakes (size 1 and size 4) or 3 Victoria sponge cakes (size 2 and size 3)

1.1kg (2lb 7oz) fondant icing

350g (12oz) modelling fondant

yellow, egg yellow and brown food colouring paste

275g (10oz) continental butter cream (for the Victoria sponge filling)

5 tablespoons apricot glaze

175g (6oz) royal icing

egg white or gum arabic

primrose yellow sparkle powder

black food colouring pen

Equipment:

5-6 cocktail sticks

30 cm (12 inch) round cake board

pastry brush

small piping nozzle

large shell nozzle

fine paintbrush

large and medium daisy cutter

1 foam sheet

daisy leaf cutter

blossom plunger cutter

small piece of voile net

Colour:

Fondant icing: 275g (10oz) bright yellow, 825g (1lb 13oz) pale yellow

Modelling fondant: 175g (6oz) golden brown (brown with a touch of egg yellow), 150g (5oz) white, 25g (1oz) cream (a touch of yellow)

1 Cover the cake board with the bright yellow fondant, reserving the trimmings, and leave to dry.

2 Slice the tops flat on all the cakes. If you have used the Victoria sponge recipe, split and fill each cake with the continental butter cream. Brush the surface of each cake with apricot glaze.

3 Starting with the largest cake, cover each cake with the pale yellow fondant icing. Place the cakes on top of each other on the board.

4 Pipe white royal icing shells round the base of each cake, leaving a 5 cm (2 inch) gap on the bottom cake where the teddy is going to sit.

5 Make the 2 teddies with the golden brown modelling fondant. For each body, roll a ball with 40g (1½oz) of the fondant and indent a line on the tummy with a cocktail stick. With the remaining fondant, roll 2 balls for the heads, model 4 legs, 4 arms and 4 ears and stick on with a little egg white or gum arabic. Stick the teddies on to the cake with a dab of royal icing. Use the cream

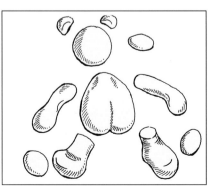

modelling fondant to model 2 noses and 4 patches for the bottom of the feet. Stick on to the teddies with egg white or gum arabic.

6 Using 50g (2oz) of the white modelling fondant, model the piping bag. Stick it to the side of the cake next to the teddy, using a little royal icing. Remove teddy's arms and place round the piping bag and, if necessary stick back in place with a little royal icing.

7 To make the daisies, roll out the remaining white modelling fondant and cut with the daisy cutters, one at a time, until you have 10 large and 16 medium daisies. Indent each petal with a cocktail stick. Place each daisy on the foam and, using the end of a paintbrush, push the centre into the foam to shape the daisy. Leave to dry upside down. Cut 2-3 leaves with the daisy leaf cutter and leave to dry. Cut 50-60 blossoms with the blossom cutter.

8 Roll the bright yellow fondant trimmings into 26 small balls, to form the pollen for each daisy. Push each ball on to the voile net to indent the pattern, then stick in the centre of the daisies with a little egg white or gum arabic. Model a little bow for the top of the piping bag and stick in place.

9 Leave the cake and the flowers to dry for at least 8 hours, or overnight. Stick all the flowers in place with royal icing and dust each daisy with the sparkle powder. Draw the faces with the black food colouring pen.

Football Crazy

A cake for anybody who's football mad, but you'd better tell them this football is for eating, not for kicking around!

You will need:

2 light fruit or healthy sponge cakes (size 2)

900g (2lb) fondant icing

125g (4oz) royal icing

6 tablespoons desiccated coconut

green, black and red food colouring paste

5 tablespoons apricot glaze

egg white or gum arabic

Equipment:

3-4 cocktail sticks

25 cm (10 inch) round cake board

pastry brush

1 sheet of card

fine paintbrush

5 cm (2 inch) plain circle cutter

garrett frill cutter

Colour:

Royal icing: 125g (4oz) green

Fondant icing: 675g (1½lb) white, 150g (5oz) black, 75g (3oz) red

1 Cover the cake board with a layer of the green royal icing and the desiccated coconut that has been coloured green (see page 24 on how to colour coconut). Set aside and leave to dry for at least 2 hours.

2 Slice the tops flat on both cakes so that they are level.

3 Stick the cakes together with a layer of apricot glaze.

4 If the 2 cakes do not make a perfectly round shape, separate and trim a little further to get as good a shape as possible. Brush a thin layer of apricot glaze all over the surface of the cake to help the fondant icing shapes stick.

5 Make the 2 templates with the piece of card. These templates are offered as a near perfect guide but you may still have to adjust your cut-out fondant shapes, both black and white very slightly, depending on the shape and size of your particular cake.

6 Using the 6-sided template, cut out 5 white fondant shapes. As a guide, place the 5-sided template directly on to the top of the ball cake and stick the 5 white fondant shapes round it, making sure that the top 2 sides of each of the shapes join up with one another exactly, as above.

7 For the second row, cut 5 more 6-sided shapes and join each one to the bottom of the first row. Place the cake on the cake board, slightly towards the back to leave enough room to drape the scarf.

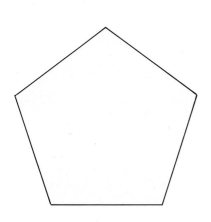

Five-sided template

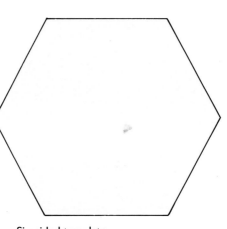

Six-sided template

8 For the third row, cut 5 more 6-sided shapes and join all of them to the second row, leaving enough space for a 5-sided shape.

9 For the fourth row, cut 5 more 6-sided shapes and join each one to the bottom of the third row tucking under the ball, if necessary.

10 Roll out the black fondant and using the template cut 11 5-sided shapes, a few at a time, and put in place on the cake, as shown above.

11 With the tip of a good sharp knife, indent tiny stitches along each join, as neatly and evenly as possible.

12 Roll out 175g (6oz) white fondant and cut a scarf measuring about 50 x 6 cm (20 x 2¹/₂ inches). Make cuts at each end for the tassles. Cover immediately with a polythene bag to prevent the icing from drying out while you make the stripes.

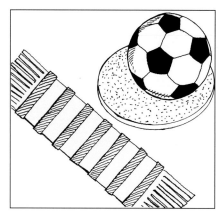

13 Roll out the red fondant, cut 7-8 strips of equal width and stick on to the scarf with a little egg white or gum arabic. Trim, then wrap the scarf round the football.

14 To make the rosette, cut a 5 cm (2 inch) circle out of the white fondant trimmings. Using the garrett frill cutter, cut out and make a frill and stick round the edge of the white circle with a little egg white or gum arabic. Cut out 2 ribbons and stick underneath the rosette. Cut a strip of red fondant and arrange round the edge of the garrett frill to disguise the join.

15 Leave the cake to dry for at least 8 hours, or overnight.

16 Paint the number 1 on the rosette with food colouring paste that has been watered down slightly.

Alternative designs:

If your football team's colours are not red and white, simply colour the correct fondant icing quantities with the appropriate colour combination and use instead. You could also colour the rosette in the same colours as well, or just use attractive complementary colours. Another fun alternative to try would be to make a referee's whistle on a piece of string. This would be easy to model, with the left-over fondant icing. Use about 25g (1 oz) of icing to model the whistle and approximately the same quantity to roll a long thin sausage shape for the string. Place on the cake board in front of the football in place of the rosette.

Rag Doll

With her sweet-natured expression, this pretty, little dolly cake is perfect for any small girl's special day.

You will need:

5 Madeira cakes (size 3, size 4, size 5, size 6)

1.35kg (3lb) fondant icing

350g (12oz) butter cream

350g (12oz) royal icing

20g (³/₄oz) modelling fondant

pink, blue, flesh, black and brown food colouring paste

egg white or gum arabic

pink dusting powder

Equipment:

5-6 cocktail sticks

25 cm (10 inch) petal shaped cake board

35 cm (14 inch) greaseproof paper circle

fluted or plain 7 cm (3 inch) circle cutter

1 skewer

No. 4 piping nozzle

fine paintbrush

primrose flower cutter

small piece of foam

small piece of voile net

Colour:

Fondant icing: 450g (1lb) pink, 625g (1lb 6oz) blue, 275g (10oz) flesh

Royal icing: 350g (12oz) brown

Modelling fondant: 15g (¹/₂oz) pink, 5g (¹/₄oz) white

1 Cover the cake board with half of the pink fondant and leave to dry.

2 Slice the tops flat on all the cakes.

3 Place the 1.2 litre (2 pint) bowl cake on top of the 15 cm (6 inch) cake. To mark the arms, make a cut about 1 cm (¹/₂ inch) deep, slicing downwards and curving inwards from the top, stopping at the bottom of the bowl cake. Mark the back of the arm by cutting a similar curving line 5 cm (2 inches) behind the first cut. Repeat on the opposite side.

4 Slice the front and back flat and trim around to the arms.

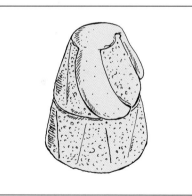

5 Slice out a small piece of cake directly underneath each hand, as above.

6 Trim the edges off the arms and any angles left around the cake. Spread 125g (4oz) of the butter cream in the layer. Place on the cake board.

7 Cut the mug cake into 3 equal slices, then cut one of the slices into 2 half

circles. For the legs, cut the ends off each half circle and stick in place with butter cream. For the shoes, trim the other two circles slightly to make oval shapes. Stick in place with butter cream. Spread a thin layer of butter cream all over the cake to help the fondant stick.

8 To make the head, sandwich the two 8 cm (3¹/₂ inch) bowl cakes together with butter cream and trim the front flat for the face. Spread a thin layer of butter cream all over and set aside.

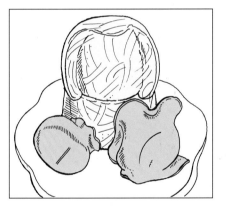

9 Roll out the remaining pink fondant and cut in half. Cover dolly's shoes, tucking the fondant underneath, and trim the tops, as shown above. Mark the heels with a knife. With the pink fondant trimmings, model a bow, and make the hairband by rolling a sausage shape then joining the ends with a little egg white or gum arabic. Set them aside and leave to dry.

10 Take 2 small pieces of blue fondant, each about the size of a marble, and press on to the top of each arm to pad out the sleeves.

11 Roll out the blue fondant and place the greaseproof paper circle on top. Cut around the paper, then lift the fondant by sliding both hands underneath and place over the top of the cake, letting it drape naturally to make the folds in the dress. Cut out a space for the arms. Mark the sleeve detail with a cocktail stick. If any small cracks appear in the fondant, rub gently with your fingers to remove them.

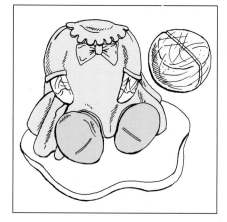

12 With the blue fondant trimmings, cut a circle using the fluted or plain 7 cm (3 inch) cutter for the collar. Stick in place with a little egg white or gum arabic, as shown above. Stick the bow in place, pushing up the collar slightly so that it fits comfortably.

13 Roll out 225g (8oz) of the flesh-coloured fondant and cover the doll's face. Tuck the fondant around the whole head, making the joins at the back. Don't worry if the back looks untidy as it will be covered completely by the hair.

14 Put the doll's head on the cake and push the skewer down through the top of the head. Model a small ball for the nose. Mark the mouth with a cocktail stick. Cover the arms with the remaining flesh-coloured fondant.

15 Colour a tiny amount of the fondant trimmings black and model 2 eyes. Stick in place with a little egg white or gum arabic.

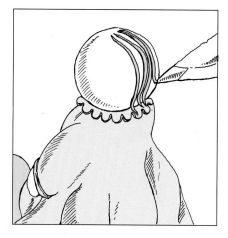

16 With the brown royal icing start piping the hair, using the No. 4 nozzle. Don't be tempted to overfill your piping bag as it will be difficult to handle and increases the chance of the bag bursting. Pipe from the top downwards, making sure each strand is completely attached to the head. If any royal icing is left unattached, it may break off as it dries. Pipe a layer of strands all around the head before you start to build up the thickness. At the last layer, start piping from the bottom upwards, this helps to get a neat finish on the ends of the hair strands. Gently put the hairband in place and pipe strands of hair coming out to make the top-knot.

17 Roll out the pink modelling fondant and cut out 6 flowers using the primrose flower cutter. Mark the lines on the petals with a cocktail stick, then place each flower on to the foam, push the end of the paintbrush into the centre to indent. With the white modelling fondant roll 6 tiny balls and press onto the voile net, this marks the pattern for the pollen on to the balls. Stick each ball into the centre of the flowers using a little egg white or gum arabic. Leave to dry, with the cake, for at least 8 hours or overnight.

18 Put a little of the pink dusting powder on your fingertip and rub a little on dolly's cheeks to give her a slight blush.

Alternative designs:

To make this pretty cake slightly different, you could alter her colour scheme by just reversing the pink and blue. Alternatively, choose completely different colouring, such as a yellow dress with green trimmings. You could also make her hair a different colour, either a flaming redhead or a bubbly blonde. Of course, you could always match the colour of her hair and clothes to the girl you are making it for!

Right: Rag doll

Golf Bag

You are bound to surprise your favourite golfer at the 19th hole with this fantastic cake!

YOU WILL NEED:
1 Madeira cake (size 1)
900g (2lb) fondant icing
650g (1lb 7oz) modelling fondant
125g (4oz) royal icing
6 tablespoons desiccated coconut
green, red and black food colouring
  paste
450g (1lb) butter cream
egg white or gum arabic
10 silver dragees
silver lustre powder
2 teaspoons clear alcohol, eg
  vodka or gin

EQUIPMENT:
3-4 cocktail sticks
25 cm (10 inch) round cake board
10 cm (4 inch) plain circle cutter
fine paintbrush
5 skewers
medium paintbrush

COLOUR:
Royal icing: 125g (4oz) green
Fondant icing: 825g (1lb 13oz)
  white, 75g (3oz) red

1 Cover the cake board with the green royal icing and the coconut coloured green (see page 24). Leave to dry for at least 2 hours.

2 Slice the top off the cake so that it is completely flat.

3 Trim 1 cm ($^{1}/_{2}$ inch) off 2 opposite sides to remove the crust, then cut the cake exactly in half. Sandwich the 2 halves with 275g (10 oz) of the butter cream.

4 Slice 2.5 cm (1 inch) off one end and cut out a 10 cm (4 inch) circle, this is for the golf bag base, as shown above.

5 Cut 2.5 cm (1 inch) off the other end and use butter cream to stick on to the cake on a side without a join, near the base, for the zip compartment. Trim to make a slight inward curve at the bottom. On the opposite side at the top of the cake, cut out a piece of cake 4 cm (1$^{1}/_{2}$ inches) in length and 2 cm ($^{3}/_{4}$ inch) in depth, curving outwards at the bottom.

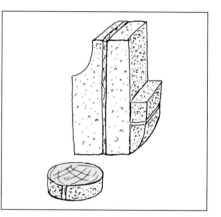

6 Spread butter cream on the 10 cm (4 inch) circle, then place the golf bag on to it. Trim away a little cake to round off the corners, then spread a thin layer of butter cream all over the cake to help the fondant stick.

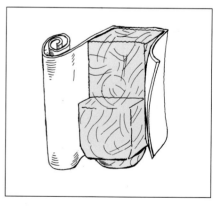

7 Roll out the white fondant icing into an oblong measuring at least 23 x 48 cm (9 x 19 inches) and cut the bottom straight. Roll up the fondant and place it against the golf bag with the straight edge at the bottom, then unroll the fondant around the bag. Trim to level the top, then place the cake on the cake board.

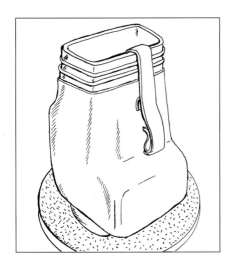

14 Mix a small quantity of the silver lustre powder with the clear alcohol and, using the medium paintbrush, paint the golf clubs and the skewers silver.

8 With 200g (7oz) of the white modelling fondant, roll and cut out a piece measuring at least 4 x 40 cm (1½ x 16 inches). Dampen the rim of the golf bag with a little egg white or gum arabic, then stick the strip in place to make the top. Cut 2 thin strips of the same length and stick them round the top. Cut 2 straps for the bag, 2 cm (¾ inch) in width, one 14 cm (5½ inches) long and the other 16 cm (6½ inches); stick in place, as shown above.

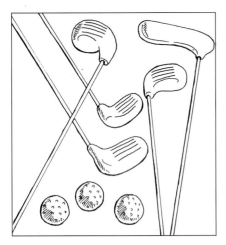

9 Model 3 irons, 1 club and 1 putter using 50g (2oz) each of the white modelling fondant. Dampen the end of each skewer and push into the bottom of the clubs. Mark the lines with a knife, then lay them flat to dry for at least 8 hours.

10 Model 3 golf balls with 50g (2oz) each and indent with the end of a paintbrush or skewer.

11 With the red fondant, cut the design for the sides and stick on with a little egg white or gum arabic. Cut a thin strip 30 cm (12 inches) long and stick round the base of the cake.

12 With the black fondant, cover inside the top of the golf bag. Cut all the trims and stick in place with a little egg white or gum arabic. Stick all the silver dragees in place, 6 round the top of the bag, 2 at the top of the strap and 2 on the zip compartment, then leave the cake to dry for at least 8 hours, or overnight.

13 Gently push all of the golf clubs into the top of the golf bag, allowing the putter and the club to rest on the top of the bag.

Alternative designs:

For a luminous variation, try colouring the balls a vibrant green and orange. You won't be able to get them completely luminous, but they should be pretty bright!
You could also create a different design for the golf bag, perhaps cut out small star shapes and stick them on to the bag at random using a little egg white or gum arabic. Finally, you can always colour the bag itself from dark blue to pale yellow!

Messy Teenager

Present this cake to your teenager and hope they feel guilty enough to clean up their room!

You will need:
1 Madeira cake (size 2)
1.3kg (2lb 13oz) fondant icing
525g (1lb 3oz) modelling fondant
blue, brown, egg yellow, red, black, lilac and flesh food colouring paste
350g (12oz) butter cream
2 teaspoons royal icing
black, green, red and brown food colouring pens
brown dusting powder
egg white or gum arabic

Equipment:
8-10 cocktail sticks
25 x 35 cm (10 x 14 inch) oblong cake board
crimper
fine paintbrush
ruler
No. 3 piping nozzle

Colour:
Fondant icing: 425g (15oz) bright blue, 650g (1lb 7oz) pine brown (brown with a touch of egg yellow), 200g (7oz) red
Modelling fondant: 75g (3oz) black, 75g (3oz) flesh, 200 g (7oz) white, 50g (2oz) yellow, 75g (3oz) dark blue, 25g (1oz) lilac
Royal icing: 2 teaspoons cream (a little egg yellow)

1 Cover the cake board with 300g (11oz) of the bright blue fondant icing. Make small even cuts with a sharp knife all round the edge for the carpet frill. Gently push the crimper into the icing and crimp a line following the frill. Leave to dry.

2 Slice the top off the cake to make it completely flat.

3 Cut the cake exactly in half length-ways and put one on top of the other. Sandwich the cakes together with about 225g (8oz) of the butter cream.

4 Cut a 2 cm ($^3/_4$ inch) deep horizontal slice from the foot of the bed, 8 cm ($3^1/_2$ inches) long. Move this piece to the other end of the bed for the head-board shelf. Cut one-third off and place this on top for the high shelf. Spread butter cream between the shelf layers.

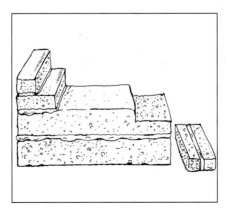

5 Trim 2 cm ($^3/_4$ inch) off the end of the chest of drawers to shorten it slightly, as shown above, then spread a thin layer of butter cream all over the cake to help the fondant stick.

6 Roll out a quarter of the pine brown fondant icing and place the back of the cake down on to it. Cut round it, then gently lift on to the cake board.

7 Measure and cut pieces of pine brown fondant to fit the 2 ends of the bed, the shelf drops and the top of the chest of drawers.

8 Measure and cut a piece of fondant to fit the front of the chest of drawers and mark the drawers, using a cocktail stick and a ruler. Model 6 handles and stick in place with a little egg white.

9 Cut a cupboard door to fit under the 2 headboard shelves and indent the louvre panels with a sharp knife. Measure the width of the remaining uncovered cupboards and cut 3 doors of equal size. Again, indent the louvre panels with a sharp knife. Set one door aside to dry and stick the other 2 in place, leaving the space in the centre.

10 With half the black modelling fondant, cover the empty door space.

11 Cover the top of the bed with the blue fondant and rub the edges to round them off to make the 'tucked-in' sheet. Make a pillow with a dent in the middle ready for the body to rest in.

12 With the red fondant, cut out the cover slightly larger than the bed. Set aside and cover with a polythene bag. Using the trimmings, roll a sausage shape and press down on the bed for the outline of the legs.

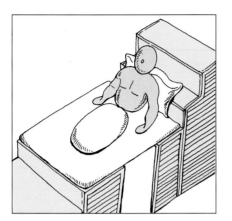

13 Take two-thirds of the flesh-coloured modelling fondant and roll into a ball. Flatten it slightly and cut 2 arms. Shape the arms and hands, working quite quickly before the icing starts to dry, and mark the chest with a cocktail stick. Roll a ball for the head and a tiny one for the nose. Stick the nose in place and indent the smile with a cocktail stick. Stick the body on to the pillow with a little egg white or gum arabic and put the red cover on, letting it reach half-way up the chest. Lift out the arms and press down gently on the cover. Stick the head in place.

14 Stick the dried louvre door in an open position with a little egg white or gum arabic.

15 With the white modelling fondant, make the boy's eyes, an open crisp packet, 3 toy boxes, a football, 2 plates (cut out with the bottom of the piping nozzle), 2 half-eaten sandwiches, 3 cups, 19 pages (9 screwed up), 4 socks and 4 oblong shapes for the inside of the books. Drape a piece of fondant over the top of the open louvre door and stick 2 pieces on the front of the second drawer.

16 Cut a square of yellow modelling fondant and screw it up. Stick on the middle of the open cupboard. Make a book cover by placing one of the oblong book shapes on the yellow fondant, cutting the top and bottom to fit, then wrapping the fondant round the front. Make 8-10 tiny crisps.

17 With the dark blue modelling fondant, make the jeans and fold them backwards. Make a book cover as before and screw up a small piece of fondant for the messy cupboard.

18 With the remaining red fondant, make covers for the last 2 books. Model 2 boxing gloves, and stick a small piece of fondant on the front of the bottom drawer.

19 To make the open book, take the lilac modelling fondant and cut an oblong shape. Fold it in half, open, then lay it face down on some of the pages on the chest of drawers. Roll a toy ball for the cupboard and model a pair of boxer shorts.

20 With the remaining black modelling fondant, make a ghetto blaster and earphones. Cut small oblong shapes for the tapes and indent 2 circles on them with the tip of the piping nozzle. Model 2 shoes and a pair of boxer shorts. Mix some black fondant with the brown trimmings until it is streaky and stick in place as if it were spilling down the side of the bed from a tipped-over cup.

21 Roll out the brown trimmings, and cut an oblong shape for the towel on the floor.

22 Cut a tie from the blue fondant trimmings and lay it over the open cupboard door.

23 With the cream coloured royal icing, and the No. 3 piping nozzle, pipe the hair and eyebrows.

24 Leave the cake to dry for at least 8 hours, or overnight.

25 With the food colouring pens, draw the eyes, patterns on the socks, toy details, sandwich fillings and the writing on the papers. Dust the clothes with the brown dusting powder to make them look dirty.

Right: Messy teenager

Pink Piggy

Simple to make and decorate, this cake could make the perfect birthday or Valentine's gift.

You will need:

2 light fruit or healthy sponge cakes (size 2)
1.15kg (2lb 9oz) fondant icing
yellow and pink food colouring paste
5 tablespoons apricot glaze
egg white or gum arabic
black food colouring pen

Equipment:

3-4 cocktail sticks
30 cm (12 inch) round cake board
pastry brush
fine paintbrush
large blossom plunger cutter
yellow ribbon

Colour:

Fondant icing: 300g (11oz) yellow,
850g (1lb 14oz) pink

1 Cover the cake board with the yellow fondant and mark the lines for the straw with a knife. Leave to dry.

2 Slice the tops flat on both cakes and stick the cakes together with half of the apricot glaze.

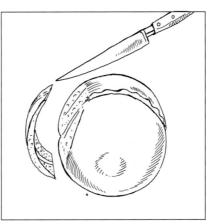

3 With the join horizontal, trim 5 mm (¹/₄ inch) off each side to make a slightly oval shape, as above. Brush the remaining apricot glaze over the surface of the cake to help the fondant stick.

4 Roll out 600g (1lb 5oz) of the pink fondant and cover the entire cake. To get the fondant to fit neatly round the bottom, stretch the folds slightly, then smooth downwards with the palm of your hand. Place the cake on the cake board.

5 With 50g (2oz) of pink fondant, roll a ball for the snout, then stick on the front of the cake with a little egg white or gum arabic. Push the end of a paintbrush into it to mark the nostrils. Mark the smile with a cocktail stick.

6 Model each ear from a 50g (2oz) piece of pink fondant, then model 2 feet weighing 25g (1oz) each. Roll a thin sausage shape for the curly tail. Stick all in place with a little egg white or gum arabic, as shown above.

7 With the pink fondant trimmings, model 3-5 baby piggies, using a cocktail stick to mark the nostrils on the snout.

8 Add a little more pink colouring to 15g (¹/₂oz) of pink fondant and cut out 5 flowers with the blossom plunger cutter. Stick these flowers on top of piggy's head with egg white or gum arabic. Make the flower centres from the yellow fondant trimmings. Stick on the yellow-coloured ribbon decoratively, in a pretty bow just above one of the ears.

9 Leave the cake to dry for at least 8 hours, or overnight.

10 Draw the eyes on the big pig and all the small pigs with the black food colouring pen.

The Old Woman in the Shoe

This cake is a nursery rhyme favourite of my children, especially when it is sliced up and being eaten!

You will need:

2 Madeira cakes (size 1) or quick mix cakes (size 3)
1.45kg (3lb 4oz) fondant icing
300g (11oz) modelling fondant
150g (5oz) royal icing
pink, blue, black, green and flesh food colouring paste
650g (1lb 7oz) butter cream
egg white or gum arabic
black food colouring pen

Equipment:

8-10 cocktail sticks
30 cm (12 inch) round cake board
fine paintbrush
teardrop-shaped cutter
blossom plunger cutter
No. 2 and No. 4 piping nozzles
ruler
small heart cutter

Colour:

Fondant icing: 375g (13oz) lilac (pink with a touch of blue), 750g (1lb 11oz) grey, 225g (8oz) dark blue, 75g (3oz) pale pink, 25g (1oz) dark grey
Modelling fondant: 75g (3oz) pink, 125g (4oz) blue, 75g (3oz) flesh, 25g (1oz) white
Royal icing: 75g (3oz) green, 50g (2oz) white

1 Cover the cake board with 275g (10oz) of the lilac fondant icing and leave to dry. Slice the tops completely flat on both cakes.

2 Cut both cakes exactly in half. Place 3 of the halves on top of each other and cut the remaining cake into 3 pieces measuring 12 x 12 cm (5 x 5 inches), 9 x 12 cm (3½ x 5 inches) and 3.5 x 12 cm (1½ x 5 inches). Place the smaller cakes one on top of the other at one end of the large cake; the 2 smallest cakes should be placed lengthways.

3 Each layer should measure no more than 2.5-4 cm (1-1½ inches) in depth. If any of them do, trim a little further. Spread butter cream between all the layers.

4 With your knife, cut a curve on the front of the shoe where the laces are to go and another for the insteps on either side of the boot.

5 To round the toe area, slice off and trim the corners. Cut out a piece from under the toe to make it look as if it is turning up slightly. Trim round to the instep and up to the beginning of the roof to round off the angles.

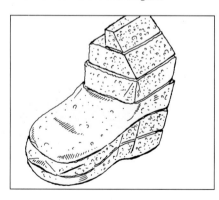

6 Cut a pointed roof by trimming off the corners from the top 2 layers. Turn these corners over and fill in the gaps.

7 To outline the bottom of the roof, slice out about 5 mm (¼ inch) from the 2 sides and at the back. Round the heel by trimming off the corners.

8 Level with the bottom of the roof, cut an archway in the front of the shoe for the window and trim out a little cake to a depth of about 1 cm (½ inch) to make room for the old woman.

9 To help the fondant stick and fill any gaps, spread a thin layer of butter cream all over the cake.

10 Roll out about 150g (5oz) of the grey fondant and cover the front of the shoe from the roof to the top of the toe to make the shoe tongue.

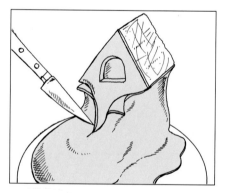

11 Roll out the remaining grey fondant and cover the shoe from the base of the roof level downwards, wrapping the fondant around and making the join at the back. Pull up the loose fondant on top of the tongue and cut out a 'v', as shown above. Trim at the roof level. Mark the shoe creases with a knife and mark the holes for the laces by pushing in with the end of a paintbrush.

12 Cut out the doorway and indent the surround with a knife. Make the steps by cutting 2 thick strips of grey fondant trimmings, one wider than the other.

13 Cut a triangle to fit the back of the roof with the grey fondant trimmings and rub the join smooth.

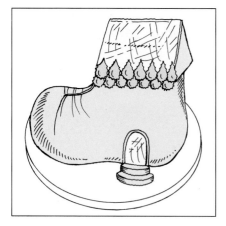

14 Take the remaining lilac fondant and grey fondant trimmings, 25g (1oz) of the dark blue and all the pale pink fondant and knead them together until the colours are just starting to mix. Roll out and cut 92 tiles with the teardrop-shaped cutter. Starting from the bottom of the roof, stick a line of 7 tiles in place. The second row of 6 tiles should overlap the first. Each side should have 7 rows. Roll a sausage shape and flatten slightly to make the ridge tiles at the top. Indent the bottom of the sausage shape slightly with a paintbrush and place on the roof. Mark the tiles with a knife.

15 With the remaining mixed colour fondant, cut out 80-90 blossom flowers with the blossom plunger cutter. Push in the centre of each blossom the tip of the No. 2 nozzle. Leave to dry.

16 With the remaining dark blue fondant, roll sausage shapes to make the laces, cut a patch for the toe and model the square chimney pot. Mark a tartan design on the patch with a knife. Cut a piece of fondant to fit the door opening and indent the lines with a ruler. Cut a small heart shape out of the middle of the door then stick the door in place. Model a small handle. For the 3 windows, cut strips of dark blue fondant measuring 6 cm (2$\frac{1}{2}$ inches) in length for the sills and 8 cm (3$\frac{1}{2}$ inches) in length for the arches. Stick in place on the shoe with a little egg white or gum arabic. Draw the window panes and handles with the black food colouring pen, pressing lightly as the fondant may still be a little soft.

17 With the dark grey fondant, cover the inside of the front window. Cut a small heart shape and insert in the door.

18 With the green royal icing and the No. 4 piping nozzle, pipe the rambling flower bush. The leaves are piped with a greaseproof paper piping bag with a small 'v' cut in the end. Stick all the blossom made earlier on to the bush and scattered on and around the shoe.

19 Divide the pink modelling fondant into 4 equal pieces. Model 3 baby nightgowns, then roll out the piece and cut out 2 curtains. Press the No. 4 piping nozzle into them to make holes for a lacy design and stick in place at the front window with the egg white or gum arabic. Model the broom brush, indenting the lines with a sharp knife.

20 Divide the blue modelling fondant into 5 equal pieces. Model 4 baby nightgowns and the old woman's chest and arms.

21 With the flesh-coloured modelling fondant, roll 8 balls for the heads, 14 hands, 14 small feet and 8 tiny noses. Indent the mouths with the tip of the No. 4 piping nozzle.

22 With the white modelling fondant, roll a very thin sausage shape for the broom handle and model the top of the

broom brush. Roll out a tiny piece to make the top of the old woman's apron, as shown above.

23 Stick everything in place with the white royal icing and the No. 2 nozzle. Pipe the old woman's hair, apron straps and small dots around her neck and sleeves. Pipe the babies' hair. Leave the cake to dry for at least 8 hours, or overnight.

24 With the black food colouring pen, draw the eyes and the eyebrows.

Humpty Dumpty

All the king's horses and all the king's men won't be able to put Humpty together again after he's been eaten!

You will need:

3 light fruit cakes (size 1, size 3)
1.4kg (3lb 2oz) fondant icing
75g (3oz) royal icing
blue, black, egg yellow, red, yellow and green food colouring paste
5 tablespoons apricot glaze
egg white or gum arabic
black food colouring pen
red dusting powder
gold lustre powder
few drops of clear alcohol, eg vodka or gin

Equipment:

7-8 cocktail sticks
25 cm (10 inch) square cake board
pastry brush
ruler
fine paintbrush
blossom plunger cutter
No. 2 piping nozzle

Colour:

Fondant icing: 450g (1lb) blue, 675g (1lb 7oz) grey, 150g (5oz) cream (a touch of egg yellow), 50g (2oz) white, 50g (2oz) red, 25g (1oz) black, 25g (1oz) yellow
Royal icing: 50g (2oz) green, 25g (1oz) yellow

1 Cover the cake board with 300g (11oz) of the blue fondant and leave to dry.

2 Slice the tops off all the cakes so they are completely flat. Cut the square cake exactly in half and place the 2 halves one on top of the other, sticking together with a little apricot glaze.

3 Stick the small bowl cake on top of the mug cake with a little apricot glaze, then brush a thin layer of apricot glaze all over the cakes to help the fondant stick.

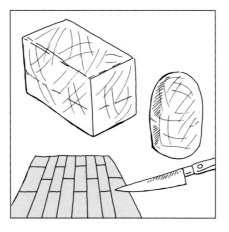

4 Using a quarter of the grey fondant, roll out and mark the horizontal lines with a ruler. Cut the bottom straight. Mark the individual bricks with a knife, then carefully turn the icing over. Place the back of the wall cake down on to the icing, lining up the bottom, then cut round it. Do the same for the sides and the front using half the fondant. Hold the cake with a cake smoother at either end if you don't want to mark the icing. Roll out the remaining grey

fondant, place the top of the cake down on to it and cut round. Place the wall cake on the cake board.

5 Cover Humpty Dumpty's head with 125g (4oz) of the cream-coloured fondant and trim halfway down. With the remaining fondant, model a tiny nose, 2 small hands and 2 circles for the bottom of the trousers. Stick the nose in place with a little egg white or gum arabic and set the hands and circles aside. Place Humpty on top of the wall.

6 Roll out the white fondant into a strip measuring 2 x 22 cm (³/₄ x 8 inches) and stick with a little egg white or gum arabic round Humpty Dumpty for his shirt collar. Model 2 circles for the eyes and stick in place. Cut the remaining white fondant in half and model 2 socks.

7 With 25g (1oz) of the blue fondant, model the top of the legs by rolling a sausage shape and bending it in half; stick in place in front of Humpty. Stick the 2 cream circles and the 2 white socks on to the bottom of the legs.

51

8 Roll out the red fondant into an oblong measuring 4 x 7 cm (1½ x 3 inches) and trim for the front of the waistcoat. Mark the lines with a knife. Press the waistcoat on to Humpty's chest, covering the tops of his legs. Model a bow tie, and stick in place with a little egg white or gum arabic. With the remaining red fondant trimmings, cut out 25-30 flowers with the blossom plunger cutter and set aside and leave to dry.

9 Roll out the remaining blue fondant into an oblong measuring 6 x 26 cm (2½ x 10½ inches) and wrap round Humpty, leaving the waistcoat uncovered, as shown above. Roll the top down to make the coat collar. Roll 2 sausage shapes for the arms and indent the creases at the elbow with a cocktail stick. Stick in place with egg white or gum arabic, with the hands at the ends, then cut 2 cuffs and place over the joins.

10 With the black fondant, model the shoes and stick in place with a little egg white or gum arabic.

11 Roll out the yellow fondant, and cut out a crown wrapping it round to make it circular and stick on Humpty's head at a jaunty angle with a little egg white or gum arabic.

12 With the green royal icing and the No. 2 piping nozzle, pipe the grass. Start at the base of the wall and move upwards, breaking off sharply to make a neat point, as above. Stick the flowers on to the board with a little royal icing. Cut a small 'V' shape in the end of a greaseproof paper piping bag and pipe the leaves with the remaining green royal icing.

13 With the yellow royal icing and the No. 2 nozzle, pipe the flower centres, the coat buttons and the buckles on the shoes. Leave the cake to dry for at least 8 hours, or overnight.

14 Draw the eyes, eyebrows and the smile with the black food colouring pen, as above. With your fingertip, gently rub a little of the red dusting powder on to Humpty's cheeks to give him a fresh, rosy look.

15 Mix the gold lustre powder with a few drops of clear alcohol, and paint the crown, the coat buttons and the shoe buckles gold.

Alternative designs:

To ring the changes, instead of using grey-coloured fondant icing for the wall, you could colour it a brick red instead. Alternatively, you could colour the blue fondant icing a rich, bright green, so Humpty would be wearing a green jacket and trousers, and the board too, would be green.

Right: Humpty dumpty

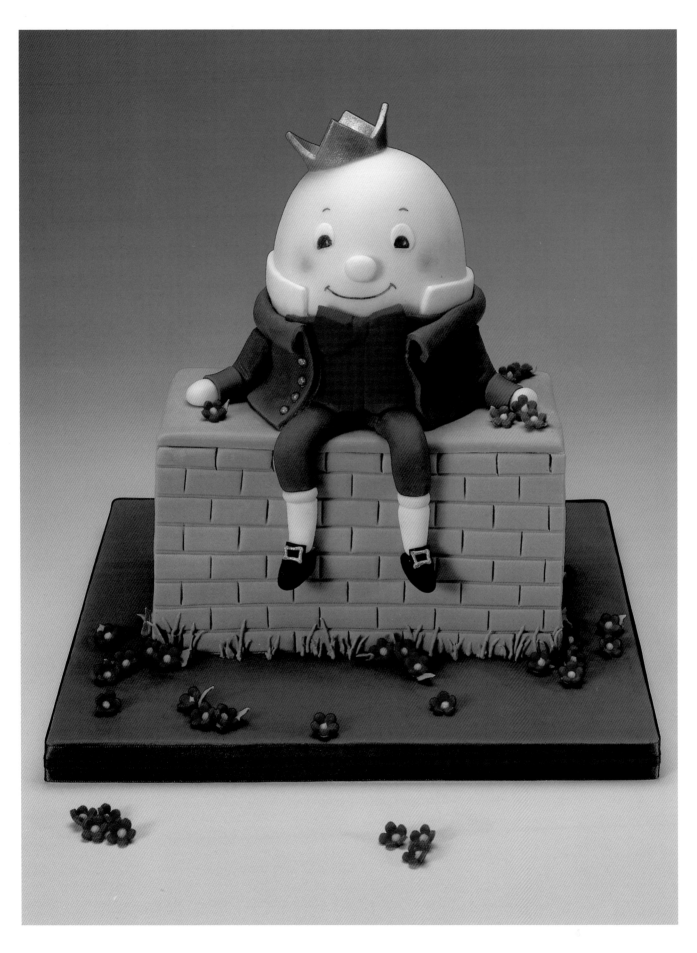

A Bottle of Bubbly

This cake is a real show stopper at a party and it's cheaper than a real bottle of champagne.

You will need:

2 Madeira cakes (size 2 and size 3)
1.55kg (3lb 7oz) fondant icing
black, green and pink food
  colouring paste
450g (1lb) butter cream
egg white or gum arabic
125g (4oz) royal icing
silver lustre powder
1-2 tablespoons vodka or gin
black food colouring pen

Equipment:

4-5 cocktail sticks
12 cm (5 inch) greaseproof paper
  circle
3 circle cutters: 7 cm (3 inch), 6 cm
  (2½ inch) and 4 cm (1½ inch)
20 cm (8 inch) round cake board
1 skewer
cotton thread
No. 2 piping nozzle
medium paintbrush
fine paintbrush
curling ribbon

Colour:

Fondant icing: 200g (7oz) pink, 200g
  (7oz) dark green, 150g (5oz)
  black, 275g (10oz) white, 725g
  (1lb 10oz) grey (a touch of black)

1 Cover the cake board with the pink fondant and leave to dry.

2 Slice the top off the 15 cm (6 inch) round cake to make it flat. Place the 12 cm (5 inch) greaseproof paper circle on the top as a guide. Trim the sides so that the top is narrower than the bottom.

3 Slice the top off the oblong cake to make it completely flat. Place the round cake at one end of the oblong, with the widest part down. Cut round it with your knife at an outward angle, following the bucket-shaped sides.

4 Using the circular cutters, cut two 7 cm (3 inch) circles and one each of the 6 cm (2½ inch) and 4 cm (1½ inch) circles at the other end of the oblong cake, as shown above. Reserve the cake trimmings to use later for the ice-cube shapes.

5 Place the bucket-shaped cake the right way up on the cake board and using a quarter of the butter cream, sandwich the layers together.

6 To tilt the bottle, trim one of the 7 cm (3 inch) circles so that it is slightly at an angle. Stick on top of the bucket with butter cream. Stick on the remaining cake circles in order of size, sandwiching them with butter cream, then trim into a bottle shape. Push the skewer into the cake down through the top of the bottle to keep it in place.

7 Spread a thin layer of butter cream all over the cake to help the fondant stick. Leave the cake to set for about 10 minutes.

8 Roll out the dark green fondant and cover the bottom half of the bottle. Rub the join together gently to close.

9 With the black fondant, roll a small sausage shape and place round the bottle, about 1 cm (½ inch) from the top. Put a piece of fondant on the top to give a rounded shape. Roll out the remaining fondant and cover the top half of the bottle completely. Close the join at the back, then twist the top slightly.

10 Roll out the white fondant and cut a label for the bottle. Stick in place with the egg white or gum arabic. Indent a circle on the neck label.

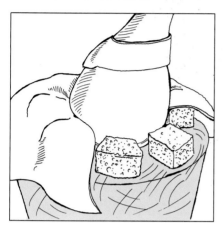

11 Cut a few of the cake trimmings into neat squares and arrange round the bottle as ice cubes. Spread a little butter cream over them to help the fondant stick, then cover with white fondant, as shown above.

12 To work out how much grey fondant to roll out, measure the widest part of the bucket with a length of cotton. Spread a little more butter cream all over the ice bucket for the fondant to stick to.

13 Roll out the grey fondant until it is the same width as the cotton measure, plus an extra 2 cm (³/₄ inch) for the rim. Roll up the fondant icing firmly, then carefully unroll it around the bucket, starting at the back. Join the edges. Trim the top of the bucket straight.

Using the cotton measure again, roll a sausage shape and wrap round the top of the bucket to make the rim. Cut 13 x 4 cm (1¹/₂ inch) circles, then cut in half. Use egg white or gum arabic to stick them on the outside of the bucket below the rim and round the base. Cut out a small shield shape and stick in the centre of the bucket. Roll out 2 small sausage shapes and stick on to the sides of the bucket for the handles.

14 Leave the cake to dry for at least 8 hours, or overnight.

15 Using the white royal icing and the No. 2 nozzle, pipe small dots all round the fondant loops on the bucket, as shown above. Leave to dry for about 30 minutes.

16 Mix the silver lustre powder with the vodka or gin. Paint the silver colour all over the ice bucket using the medium paintbrush. Using the fine paintbrush, paint a little of the silver on to the neck label. Leave to dry for 1 hour.

17 Draw on the label design with the black food colouring pen. For the finishing touch add the curling ribbon and you now have the perfect celebration novelty cake!

Alternative design:

If this cake is for a particular occasion, such as an engagement or anniversary celebration, it would be a nice idea to pipe the couple's names on to the front of the ice bucket using the white royal icing and the No. 2 nozzle. Once it has dried, you could paint over it with the silver lustre paint or leave it as it is.

At the Office

Just the cake to cheer up the grumpy boss and perhaps get round him for a pay rise?

You WILL NEED:

1 Madeira cake (size 2)
1.12kg (2lb 8oz) fondant icing
400g (14oz) modelling fondant
blue, green, black, flesh and red
    food colouring paste
350g (12oz) butter cream
egg white or gum arabic
1 teaspoon royal icing
black food colouring pen

EQUIPMENT:

5-6 cocktail sticks
30 cm (12 inch) square cake board
ruler
fine paintbrush
blossom cutter
6 white stamens

COLOUR:

Fondant icing: 450g (1lb) turquoise
    (equal quantities of blue and
    green), 675g (1½lb) grey
Modelling fondant: 50g (2oz) black,
    175g (6oz) white, 50g (2oz) flesh,
    75g (3oz) grey, 25g (1oz) red
Royal icing: 1 teaspoon grey

1 Cover the cake board with 275g (10oz) of the turquoise fondant icing. With a ruler, indent the lines for the flooring. Set aside to dry.

2 Slice the top off the cake to make it completely flat, then turn it over.

3 Cut out an oblong 12 x 19 cm (5 x 7½ inches) to make the desk. Cut the remaining cake into 6 oblong shapes each measuring 6 x 7 cm (2½ x 3 inches) to make the filing cabinets, chair back and base. See the diagram below.

4 Slice a layer in the desk cake and spread one-third of the butter cream in the middle. Sandwich the 2 halves of each filing cabinet together with butter cream.

5 Trim the short side of the chair back to make the top curve round. Cut 1 cm (½ inch) off the depth of the chair and the chair base to make them slightly smaller, then stick them together with butter cream. Spread a thin layer of butter cream over all the cakes.

6 To cover the desk, roll out about half of the grey fondant icing. Cut 2 oblong shapes to fit the front and back

of the desk, leaving them slightly short. Indent the lines with your ruler. Do the same for the sides of the desk, then stick in place, as above. Measure the corners and cut 4 legs; stick in place. Measure the top of the cake and cut the desk top slightly larger than the cake. Place the desk at one side of the cake board, towards the front.

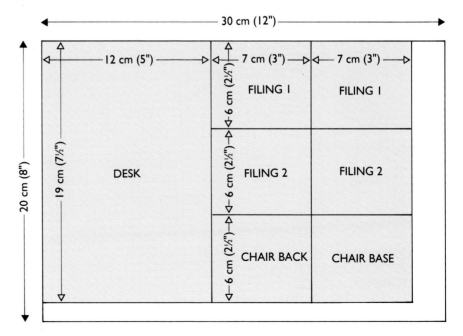

7 To cover the filing cabinets, roll out the remaining grey fondant and place the backs of the cabinets on it. Cut round them, and cover the backs, then the sides, the tops and finally the fronts, marking the lines for the drawers with a sharp knife. Roll 6 tiny balls for the drawer handles and stick in place with a little egg white or gum arabic applied with a paintbrush. Place on the cake board.

8 Roll out the remaining turquoise fondant and place one of the chair sides on it. Cut round it, and repeat for the other side. Cover the front and back of the chair with one long piece of fondant. Place the chair on the cake board, right up against the desk.

9 To make the filing trays, roll out the turquoise fondant trimmings and cut 3 oblong shapes. Turn up the ends with a knife and set aside to dry.

10 With the black modelling fondant, make 2 small circles for the printer roller and model a black tie. Set these aside to dry. With the remaining black modelling fondant, model a ball shape and stick on the chair seat with a little egg white or gum arabic. Press in with your finger to flatten the stomach.

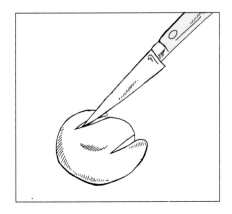

11 To make the shirt, roll 75g (3oz) of the white modelling fondant into a ball, then flatten it slightly. Cut 2 arms and soften the edges with your fingers. Stick on top of the trousers with a little egg white or gum arabic.

12 With the flesh-coloured modelling fondant, roll a ball for the head and a tiny one for the nose. Stick the nose in position with a little egg white or gum arabic and indent the mouth with a cocktail stick. Model the 2 hands, and stick on to the shirt.

13 With the grey modelling fondant, make the computer screen, keyboard, printer base and telephone. Use a sharp knife to mark the keys on the keyboard. The telephone receiver is made by rolling a sausage shape until the middle rolls thinner than the ends.

14 Roll out the remaining white modelling fondant and cut 28-30 papers. Stick these in position with a little egg white or gum arabic and pile up the 'in' trays. Cut a long strip for the printer paper and indent with a knife to mark the pages. Stick on the printer base, letting it fall to the floor. Roll a small sausage shape for the top of the printer and stick the 2 small black circles made earlier on each end with a little egg white or gum arabic. With the blossom cutter, cut 6 flowers and push the stamens through the centres. Stick in place with a little egg white or gum arabic and leave to dry upside-down. Cut out a collar for the shirt and stick in position with the black tie made earlier.

15 To make the books, roll out the white fondant trimmings quite thickly and cut 4 oblong shapes. Roll out the red modelling fondant and place 2 of the white oblong shapes on it. Cut the

top and bottom to fit, then wrap the red fondant around the white to make the book covers. Model 4 red pencils.

16 With the turquoise fondant trimmings, make 2 book covers as before. Model a vase by rolling a small ball shape then indenting the top slightly with the end of a paintbrush. Gently push the flowers into the top.

17 Leave the cake to dry for at least 8 hours, or overnight.

18 Spread the royal icing onto the head, curling the hair slightly with a cocktail stick.

19 With the black food colouring pen, write on the books and papers and make dots for the telephone buttons. Draw the eyes and the 'cross' eyebrows for a grumpy-looking boss.

Right: At *the office*

Chocolate Teddy Bear

This cake will make the ultimate gift for fellow teddy bear-mad chocoholics everywhere!

You will need:

5 Madeira cakes (size 3, size 4, size 5, size 6)
825g (1lb 13oz) fondant icing
blue, red, brown and black food colouring paste
1.35kg (3lb) chocolate butter cream
egg white or gum arabic

Equipment:

3-4 cocktail sticks
25 cm (10 inch) round cake board
skewer
round-ended knife
fork
fine paintbrush

Colour:

Fondant icing: 450g (1lb) blue, 200g (7oz) red, 175g (6oz) brown

1 Cover the cake board with 275g (10oz) of the blue fondant and leave to dry. Slice the tops off all the cakes so they are completely flat.

2 Place the large bowl cake on top of the 15 cm (6 inch) round cake. To mark the arms, make a cut about 1 cm (½ inch) deep, and continue to cut in a curving line down to the bottom of the bowl cake. Mark the back of the arm with a similar curving line, 5 cm (2 inches) behind the first line. Repeat for the other arm.

3 Make a horizontal cut about 2 cm (¾ inch) deep in the front of the cake for the top of the present, then cut out teddy's chest and a small piece above each arm. Trim the front of the present.

4 Slice downwards at the back, keeping the bottom area rounded, then trim round to the arms. Slice out a piece of cake underneath each arm, then trim the base of the cake by 5 mm (¼ inch) all the way round, cutting at an inwards angle.

5 Trim the edges off the arms and trim any angles left round the cake. Sandwich the 2 cakes with about 200g (7oz) of the chocolate butter cream, then place the cake on the cake board.

6 Cut the mug cake into 3 equal slices, then cut one of the slices into 2 semicircles. For the legs, cut the ends off each semicircle and stick in place with butter cream. For the feet, trim the other 2 circles slightly to make oval shapes, then stick in place with butter cream. Spread a thin layer of butter cream all over the cake.

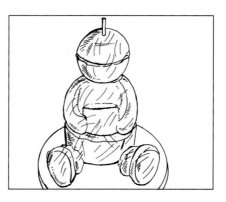

7 Sandwich the 2 small bowl cakes together with butter cream to make the head, and trim out a piece of cake to flatten the eye area. Spread a thin layer of butter cream all over the head, then place on top of the body. Push the skewer down through the top of the head to keep it in place. Roll out the red fondant and cover teddy's present.

8 With the brown fondant, roll two 25g (1oz) balls and model the ears. Press in place. Pad out teddy's nose area and his hands with 25g (1oz) pieces of fondant. Roll out the remaining brown fondant and cut 2 shapes for the pads of his feet; press in place. Model 2 eyes and set aside. Knead a little black food colouring paste into the brown fondant trimmings, model a nose and 2 pupils for the eyes, set aside.

9 Spread a thick layer of the chocolate butter cream over the feet and legs, leaving the pads uncovered, then use a fork to mark the lines for the fur. Next, cover and mark the back, the chest, the arms, and the head, leaving the inside of the ears uncovered.

10 Stick the eyes and nose in place, then mark the smile and eyebrows with a cocktail stick. Put a little butter cream on the eyes so they look more lively.

11 With the remaining blue fondant, model a parcel and teddy's bow; press the bow in place. Roll out the trimmings and cut thin strips to decorate the red parcel; stick in place with a little egg white or gum arabic. Roll out the red fondant trimmings and cut strips for the blue parcel; stick in place. Leave the cake to dry for 8 hours.

The Field Mouse Picnic

A cake to charm anyone, perhaps surprise Mum or Grandma on Mother's Day.

You will need:

1 healthy sponge cake (size 3) or Victoria sponge cake (size 1)
850g (1lb 13oz) fondant icing
675g (1½lb) modelling fondant
225g (8oz) royal icing
green, dark brown, black, egg yellow, blue, pink, lilac, golden brown and yellow food colouring paste
5 tablespoons apricot glaze
275g (10oz) continental butter cream (for Victoria sponge)
egg white or gum arabic
brown, green and red dusting powder
blue, green, brown, black and red food colouring pens
pinch of granulated sugar

Equipment:

10-12 cocktail sticks
35 cm (14 inch) petal-shaped cake board
piece of foam (optional)
pastry brush
fine paintbrush
4 cm (1½ inch) and 2.5cm (1 inch) plain circle cutters
medium paintbrush
small and medium blossom plunger cutters
no. 2 piping nozzle
piping bag
crimping tool

Colour:

Fondant icing: 350g (12oz) white, 350g (12oz) light brown, 150g (5oz) cream (a touch of egg yellow)
Modelling fondant: 75g (3oz) light brown, 200g (7oz) grey, 25g (1oz) dark grey, 75g (3oz) pink, 75g (3oz) blue, 75g (3oz) lilac, 25g (1oz) light green, 25g (1oz) golden brown, 25g (1oz) white, 25g (1oz) yellow
Royal icing: 225g (8oz) green

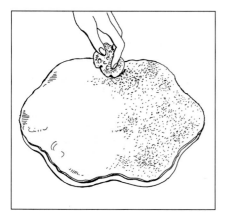

1 Spread the cake board with 175g (6oz) of the green royal icing, making it slightly thicker near the edge of the board. 'Stipple' it with a small piece of foam, then leave to dry.

2 Slice the top off the cake so it is completely flat.

3 Cut a 5 cm (2 inch) strip from one side of the cake, and another from the back, so you are left with the picnic table cake measuring 15 cm (6 inches) square and 2 strips, one longer than the other. Cut 5 cm (2 inches) off the longer strip so they are of equal length, then cut them in half to make the 4 log seats. Trim the corners to make the seats round, then brush with apricot glaze to help the fondant stick.

4 If you have used the Victoria sponge recipe, split and fill the square cake with the continental butter cream. Place the picnic table cake in the centre of the board, then brush with apricot glaze.

5 Roll out the white fondant icing and cut out a 25 cm (10 inch) square. Trim the corners to round them off, then place on the picnic table for the cloth.

6 Roll out 75g (3oz) of the light brown fondant icing and place a log seat cake on to it. Trim the sides of the icing to match the log, then roll the icing round the log and trim. With a cocktail stick, mark the lines and dents to resemble the bark. Cover the other 3 log seats in the same way. Model a twig stump and stick on with egg white, then put all the log seat cakes to one side.

7 With two-thirds of the light brown modelling fondant, roll sausage shapes and mark with a cocktail stick to make the logs and twigs; set aside.

8 Paint the 4 log seat cakes and all of the modelled logs and twigs with a little brown food colouring paste mixed with a few drops of water, then leave to dry.

9 With 25g (1oz) each of the light grey and dark grey modelling fondant, model the rocks and stones; set aside.

10 Roll out the cream-coloured fondant icing and cut out 8 circles with the 4 cm (1¹/₂ inch) circle cutter. Place these on each end of the log seat cakes.

11 Arrange the log seat cakes and all the rocks, stones, logs and twigs on the cake board, sticking in place with a little royal icing. Brush a little brown and green dusting powder on and round them, using the medium paintbrush.

12 Roll out 25g (1oz) each of the blue and pink modelling fondant and cut 60-70 small blue flowers and 30-40 medium pink flowers with the blossom plunger cutters. Push in the centre of each flower with the tip of the No. 2 nozzle.

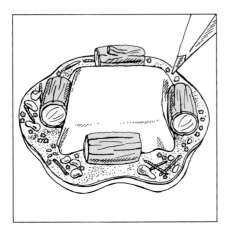

13 Pipe the long grass with green royal icing and the No. 2 nozzle. Arrange the flowers on the cake board and stick in place with the royal icing.

14 With the light grey, blue and pink modelling fondant, make the mice in various sizes and poses. All of the mice have a ball for the body and a slightly smaller ball for the head, rolled to a soft point on one side for the nose. The mice with summer hats have their ears put on after the hat is in place. Make small flattened balls for the ears then indent with your little finger. Stick on a little pink fondant and mark with a cocktail stick. Stick all the mice in place with a little royal icing, except the one on the table, which is put on after the table design is drawn. Don't make the tails yet.

15 With the remaining light brown modelling fondant, make the 2 food baskets. Take a piece about the size of a marble and roll 4 thin sausage shapes. Twist 2 together to make the handles. Cut the remaining fondant in half and roll into 2 balls. With the crimping tool held vertically, crimp all round each basket, then crimp the top edge. Push your finger into the centre to hollow it out slightly. Stick the handles in place with a little egg white or gum arabic.

16 With the lilac modelling fondant, make the plates, cups, teapot and sugar bowl. Use the 2.5 cm (1 inch) circle cutter to cut out the plates. For the cups, roll small balls and push the end of a paintbrush into the centres.

17 With the green modelling fondant, make the 2 apples and indent the top with a cocktail stick. Model 2 tiny stalks with the light brown modelling fondant trimmings and stick on the top of the apples.

18 With the golden brown modelling fondant, make a loaf of bread, a pie with a piece cut out, 6 jam tart bases with the edges marked with the tip of a cocktail stick, 5 small cakes and 1 large cake.

19 With the white modelling fondant, make 4 napkins, 1 large cake, 6 triangular sandwiches and 2 bottles.

20 With the yellow modelling fondant, make 3 cheeses with the holes marked with the tip of the No. 2 piping nozzle, the open book for the sleepy mouse and a bottle.

21 Leave everything to dry for at least 8 hours, or overnight.

22 With the food colouring pens, draw the patterns on the tablecloth, napkins and crockery. Draw the bottle labels, the sandwich and jam tart fillings, the pattern on the large white cake and the filling on the golden brown cake. Draw the pattern on each end of the log seat cakes with the brown food colouring pen. With the black pen, draw the eyes, noses and whiskers on the mice.

23 With some of the remaining grey modelling fondant, roll very thin sausage shapes for the tails and stick in place on the mice with a little egg white or gum arabic.

24 Put a tiny amount of red dusting powder on your fingertip and rub a little on to each apple.

25 Stick everything in position using a little egg white or gum arabic. Dust a little icing sugar on top of the golden brown cake and fill the sugar bowl with a pinch of granulated sugar.

Patch the Puppy

This adorable puppy dog with his cute expression will melt the heart of any animal lover.

You will need:

2 quick mix cakes (size 1 and size 5)
900g (2lb) fondant icing
egg yellow, brown, black, orange and green food colouring paste
125g (4oz) butter cream
egg white or gum arabic

Equipment:

3-4 cocktail sticks
25 x 30 cm (10 x 12 inch) oval cake board
fine paintbrush

Colour:

Fondant icing: 800g (1lb 12oz) cream (a touch of egg yellow), 90g (3¹/₂oz) brown, 5g (¹/₄oz) black, 5g (¹/₄oz) orange

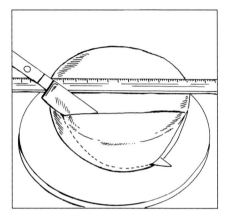

1 Place the 20 cm (8 inch) cake on the cake board with the top uppermost. Cut a 16 cm (6¹/₂ inch) slice from the back – it should be 4 cm (1¹/₂ inches) at its widest point – keeping your knife at an outward angle to create a sloping back.

2 Measure 11 cm (4¹/₂ inches) from the tail end of the cake, and mark a line with your knife down to the front of the cake. Cut the marked area away in a 1 cm (¹/₂ inch) deep horizontal slice, to make room for the head.

4 Turn the cake round and in the centre of the front, cut out a wedge of cake at a slight angle, about 6 cm (2¹/₂ inches) at the widest point to mark the separation of the front and back legs.

5 For his front paws, cut away a piece of cake about 4 cm (1¹/₂ inches) in depth and the same in length. To mark the separation of his two front paws, cut out a small 'v'-shaped piece of cake in the middle. Trim to neaten.

3 With your knife, trim Patch's back to slope gently round to where the tail is going to be, as above.

6 Trim out a small piece of cake about 1 cm (¹/₂ inch) deep to mark a place for the tail, as above.

7 Cut off all angles and trim a thin wedge between the front paws.

8 Cut out a small triangle to separate the tip of the tail and the back paw.

9 Trim from the top of the cake down to the back paw to round it off.

10 Trim the top off the bowl-shaped cake.

11 Cut out 2 narrow wedges from either side of the head to mark the ears, and do the same for the back of the ears. Trim the front to shape the jaw and round it off.

12 Slice out a piece of cake on either side of the face where the eyes are going to be and slice a little out between the eyes for the bridge of the nose.

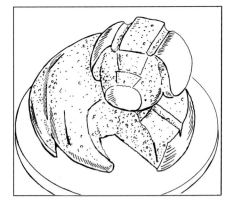

13 Mark the top of the ears by cutting out a very thin wedge, and trim the back of the head down to the neck to round it off, as shown above.

14 Spread a thin layer of butter cream over both cakes to help the fondant stick.

15 Roll out half of the cream fondant icing and cover Patch's body. Mark the front paws with a cocktail stick.

16 Roll out about half of the remaining cream fondant and cover Patch's head, tucking the icing underneath instead of trimming. Put a little butter cream on the underside and place the head on the body. With a sharp knife, cut a line for Patch's smile. With the tip of the knife, pull down the bottom lip slightly to make enough room for the tongue.

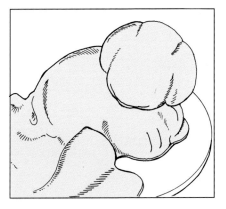

17 Thinly roll out the remaining cream fondant and drape it round Patch for the rug, as above.

18 Roll out the brown fondant and cover one ear and the tail. Model 3 patches by pressing the fondant into the palm of your hand. Using a little egg white or gum arabic, stick 1 patch on the eye and the other 2 patches on the body.

19 With a sharp knife, mark lines on all the brown patches.

20 Model a black nose, 2 black eyes and a small orange tongue. Stick everything in place with a little egg white or gum arabic.

21 Put a tiny piece of cream fondant icing on to each eye to give a little 'sparkle'.

22 Leave Patch to dry for at least 8 hours, or overnight.

23 When the cake is completely dry, paint the tartan design on the rug with brown, orange and green food colouring paste that has been watered down slightly.

Alternative designs:

If you would like to make the bone, as an extra decorative item, for the cake, take 125g (4oz) of cream-coloured fondant icing and roll it carefully into a sausage shape, keeping the ends slightly bulbous. Model the 2 ends into bone shapes and mark the line with a cocktail stick. Alternatively, you could just roll the fondant into a bouncy ball shape, or perhaps if you are feeling adventurous, a chewed slipper!

Right: Patch the puppy

Jolly Chef

Every fella likes to think he's a cordon bleu cook after just one go in the kitchen, so this is the cake for him!

YOU WILL NEED:

5 Madeira cakes (size 3, size 4, size 5, size 6)

1.6kg (3lb 10oz) fondant icing

375g (13oz) modelling fondant

175g (6oz) royal icing

blue, flesh, black, brown, red, green and egg yellow food colouring paste

450g (1lb) butter cream

egg white or gum arabic

black and blue food colouring pens

pink dusting powder

EQUIPMENT:

7-8 cocktail sticks

25 cm (10 inch) round cake board

10 cm (4 inch) diameter bowl

fine paintbrush

skewer

6 cm (2½ inch) plain circle cutter

small calyx cutter

piping bag

COLOUR:

Fondant icing: 250g (9oz) blue, 900g (2 lb) white, 250g (9oz) flesh, 250g (9oz) black

Modelling fondant: 195g (6¾oz) white, 125g (4oz) light brown, 50g (2oz) red, 5g (¼oz) green

Royal icing: 175g (6oz) cream (a touch of egg yellow)

1 Cover the round cake board with the blue fondant icing and set aside to dry. Reserve the leftover trimmings to use for the eyes.

2 Dust the small bowl with a little icing sugar. Roll out the white modelling fondant and carefully cover the outside of the small bowl. Trim, then set aside to dry.

3 Slice the tops off all the cakes so they are completely flat.

4 Place the large bowl cake on top of the 15 cm (6 inch) round cake. To mark the arms, make a cut about 1 cm (½ inch) deep, and continue to cut in a curving line down to the bottom of the bowl cake. Mark the back of the arm with a similar curving line 5 cm (2 inches) behind the first line. Repeat for the other arm.

5 Slice the front flat and trim round to the arms. Slice downwards at the back, keeping the bottom area rounded, then trim round to the arms.

6 Slice out a piece of cake directly underneath each arm, then trim at the base of the cake by about 5 mm (¼ inch) all the way round, cutting at an inwards angle. Trim the edges off the arms and trim any angles that are left round the cake.

7 Carefully sandwich the 2 cakes together with one-quarter of the butter cream and then place the cake on the cake board.

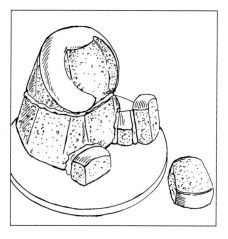

8 Cut the mug cake into 3 equal slices, then cut one of the slices into 2 semi-circles. For the legs, cut the ends off each semicircle and stick in place with butter cream. For the shoes, trim the other 2 circles slightly to make oval shapes, then stick in place with butter cream, as shown above. Spread a thin layer of butter cream all over the cake to help the fondant stick and to seal the cake to prevent crumbs.

9 Sandwich the 2 small bowl cakes together with butter cream to make the head, and trim the front flat to help shape the face. Then spread a thin layer of butter cream all over the head and set aside.

10 Roll out 300g (11oz) of the white fondant icing into a strip measuring 7 x 46 cm (3 x 18 inches) and cover the bottom part of the cake (the trousers), making the join at the front. You may want to remove the shoes for a moment while you do this, so they don't get in the way.

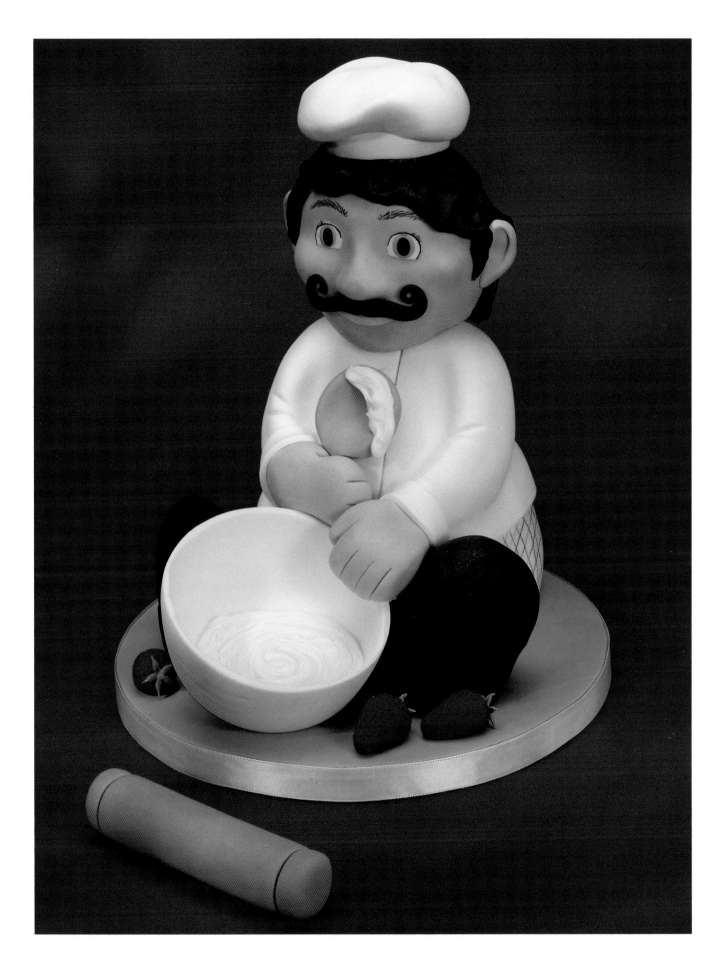

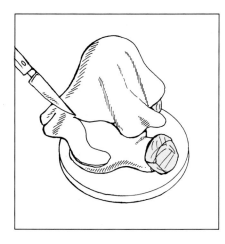

11 Roll out 350g (12oz) of the white fondant icing into a circle and cover the top part of the cake. Trim to make the jacket. Mark the sleeve creases and the jacket opening with a cocktail stick. Roll 6 small buttons and stick on the front of the jacket with a little egg white.

12 With 25g (1oz) of the flesh-coloured fondant icing, model a nose, using half and stick on the front of the head. Divide the other half into 6 pieces. Roll 3 small balls, 2 to pad out the cheeks and 1 for the chin. Roll 3 very thin sausage shapes, 2 for the eyebrows and 1 for the bottom lip. With another 25g (1oz), model 2 ears and set aside to dry. Roll out 75g (3oz) of the fondant and cover the face, smoothing out and shaping the features with your fingers. Stick the ears on with a little egg white.

13 Place the head on top of the body and push the skewer down through the top of the head to keep it in place.

14 Roll out 150g (5oz) of the black fondant icing and cut in half, then cover the shoes, marking the heels with a knife. With the trimmings, model the moustache and stick in place with a little egg white or gum arabic.

15 Roll out the remaining black fondant thickly and cover the top and back of the head. Pinch with your fingers for the hair. Pinch some down in front of the ears to make the sideburns.

16 To make the chef's hat, roll out 75g (3oz) of the white fondant icing about 1 cm (½ inch) thick and cut out the rim with the 6 cm (2½ inch) circle cutter. Model the top of the hat with 150g (5oz) of fondant. Stick in place.

17 Roll out some of the white fondant trimmings and cut out 2 eyes and a smile. Stick in place with a little egg white or gum arabic. Put 2 tiny balls of blue fondant into the palm of your hand and press to make circles for the irises; stick in place.

18 Make the rolling pin by rolling 75g (3oz) of the brown modelling fondant into a thick sausage shape and marking the ends with a cocktail stick. Make the top of the spoon by rolling three-quarters of the remaining brown fondant into a ball, then shaping it in the palm of your hand by pushing your thumb into it. Roll the remaining fondant into a small sausage shape for the spoon handle. Set aside to dry.

19 Cut the red modelling fondant into 3 equal pieces, then model 3 strawberries. Mark with the end of a cocktail stick. Cut out 3 small calyxes for the top of the strawberries with the green modelling fondant and the calyx cutter and stick in place with a little egg white or gum arabic.

20 With the remaining flesh-coloured fondant icing, model the hands and leave to dry with the cake for at least 8 hours, or overnight.

21 Gently remove the fondant from the outside of the bowl and place between the chef's legs at a slight angle. Fill a piping bag without a nozzle with the cream-coloured royal icing and squeeze most of the icing into the bowl, stirring it around. Stick the hands and the spoon in place with a little royal icing, then put some royal icing on the spoon.

22 With the black food colouring pen, draw the pupils in the eyes and the eyebrows. Draw the check pattern on the trousers with the blue food colouring pen. With your fingertip, rub a little pink dusting powder on to the chef's cheeks and his lip.

Hickory Dickory Clock

This smiley-faced clock makes a lovely cake for small children who enjoy traditional nursery rhymes.

You will need:

1 Madeira cake (size 2)
1.1kg (2lb 7oz) fondant icing
350g (12oz) modelling fondant
blue and pink food colouring paste
400g (14oz) butter cream
egg white or gum arabic
125g (4oz) royal icing
silver lustre powder
2 teaspoons vodka or gin
black food colouring pen
1 sheet leaf gelatine

Equipment:

3-4 cocktail sticks
25 cm (10 inch) square cake board
fine paintbrush
2 plain circle cutters: 7 cm (3 inch)
   and 6 cm (2½ inch)
No. 1 and No. 2 piping nozzles

Colour:

Fondant icing: 275g (10oz) white,
   825g (1lb 13oz) blue
Modelling fondant: 150g (5oz) pale
   blue, 100g (3½oz) white, 100g
   (3½oz) pink
Royal icing: 125g (4oz) pale blue

1 Cover the cake board with the white fondant icing, set aside and leave to dry thoroughly. Reserve all of the trimmings.

2 Slice the top off the cake to make it completely flat. Then turn it over so the bottom is now the top.

3 Cut the cake exactly in half lengthways. Cut one half to make two 10 x 11 cm (4 x 4½ inch) cakes. Cut the other half to make three cakes, one measuring 10 x 14 cm (4 x 5½ inches) and the other two both measuring 7 x 10 cm (3 x 4 inches). See the diagram below for clear and precise instructions.

4 Carefully trim 1 cm (½ inch) off the depth of the two 10 x 11 cm (4 x 4½ inch) size cakes to make them slightly smaller.

5 With one-third of the butter cream, stick together the two 10 x 11 cm (4 x 4½ inch) size cakes, which make the clock face and the two 7 x 10 cm (3 x 4 inch) size cakes, which make the middle of the clock. The remaining cake is the base.

6 Spread a thin layer of butter cream over each cake to help the fondant stick and to thoroughly seal the cake to prevent crumbs.

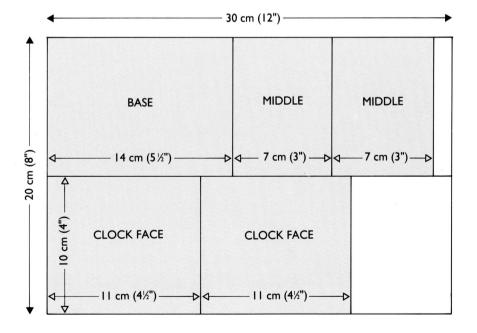

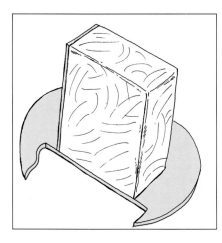

7 Roll out the blue fondant. Place the back of the base cake on the fondant and cut round it. Cover the sides, then the front, and place on the cake board. Cover the middle cake with fondant in the same way, then spread half of the remaining butter cream on the bottom of the cake and place on the centre of the base cake. Spread the top with the remaining butter cream. Cover all 4 sides and the top and bottom of the clock face with fondant, and place on top of the middle cake.

8 Measure the clock face and cut a frame out of the pale blue modelling fondant. Stick in place with egg white or gum arabic. With a knife, indent a line all the way round the middle of the frame. Cut a 7 cm (3 inch) circle of pale blue modelling fondant and cut off the top part to make the arch at the top; set aside to dry. Cut out an oblong measuring 6 x 7 cm (2½ x 3 inches) and cut out the centre to make the door

frame. Indent a line all the way round the middle and stick in place with a little egg white. Model the door handle and stick on with egg white. Model 8 decorative knobs and 2 small teardrop shapes for the weights inside the clock door; set aside to dry.

9 With the pale blue modelling fondant, cut four 2.5 cm (1 inch) wide strips and place them round the top of the base, a side at a time, overlapping them slightly. Trim the corners to make a neat join. Place thicker strips of fondant all the way round the bottom of the middle part and the base, making the join at the back.

10 For the clock face, roll out the white fondant trimmings quite thickly and cut out a 6 cm (2½ inch) circle. Indent the eyes with your index finger. Flatten the chin, pushing upwards to create a small bump for the nose. Rub the cheeks gently with your fingers to round them off and rub the edges to soften. Set aside to dry.

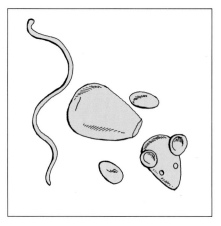

11 Make 3-4 mice using the white and pink modelling fondant. To make each mouse, roll 2 teardrop shapes, one slightly larger than the other, and stick together with a little egg white or gum arabic. Roll a thin sausage shape for the tail and flatten 2 ball shapes for the ears. Roll 2 small ball shapes for the front paws. Finally model the eyes with very tiny balls of fondant. As shown in the illustration above.

12 With the pale blue royal icing, pipe the clock numbers and hands with the No. 1 piping nozzle. Leave to dry for a few minutes, then stick the face on to the clock with a little royal icing. With the No. 2 nozzle, pipe small dots round the base, the middle and the clock face. Pipe the scrolls on the base and the arch. Pipe the lines with handles for the weights. With a little royal icing, stick on the arch at the top and stick all the decorative knobs in place. Stick on the weights at the bottom of the piped lines in the door.

13 Leave the cake to dry for at least 8 hours, or overnight.

14 Mix the silver powder with the vodka or gin to make a paste and paint it on to the weights, clock face numbers and hands, scrolls and the top of the decorative knobs.

15 With the black food colouring pen, draw the eyes, eyebrows, smile and the dots on the clock face.

16 Cut a square of leaf gelatine and wedge it into the clock door.

17 With a little royal icing, stick all the mice in place.

Right: Hickory dickory clock

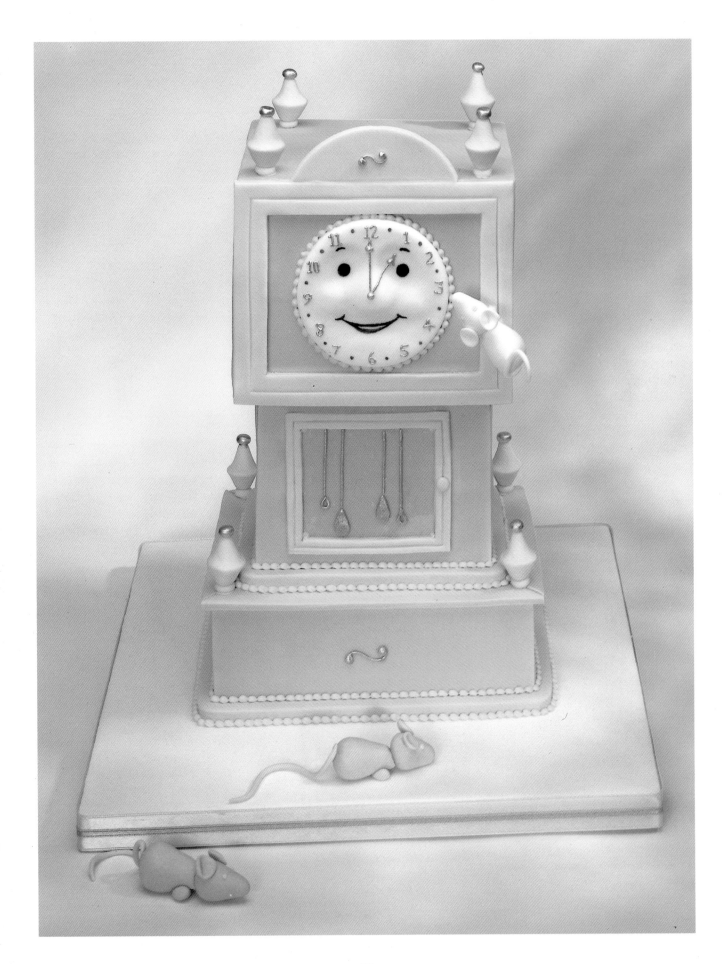

The Wicked Witch

The perfect cake for Hallowe'en, or, dare I say it, the mother-in-law's birthday?

You will need:

2 Madeira or quick mix cakes (size 2 and size 4)
925g (2lb 1oz) fondant icing
300g (11oz) modelling fondant
275g (10oz) royal icing
green, black, mauve, brown, red and egg yellow food colouring paste
450g (1lb) butter cream
egg white or gum arabic
silver snowflake lustre powder
black and red food colouring pens

Equipment:

8-10 cocktail sticks
25 cm (10 inch) round cake board
cotton thread
fine paintbrush
2 wooden skewers
5 cm (2 inch) plain circle cutter
piping bag
large size star or shell piping nozzle
No. 2 piping nozzle

Colour:

Fondant icing: 200g (7oz) green, 450g (1lb) black, 275g (10oz) mauve
Modelling fondant: 125g (4oz) black, 40g (1½oz) light green, 40g (1½oz) mauve, 25g (1oz) white, 75g (3oz) brown
Royal icing: 125g (4oz) white, 50g (2oz) red, 50g (2oz) egg yellow, 50g (2oz) black

1 Cover the cake board with the green fondant icing and leave to dry.

2 Slice the tops completely flat on both cakes.

3 Cut the oblong cake in half widthways, then cut one of the halves into 3 equal pieces. Place the bowl-shaped cake upside down on one end of the half cake and cut round it.

4 Turn the cauldron cake over and trim to a rounded shape. Sandwich the cakes together with a quarter of the butter cream, then spread a thin layer of butter cream all over the cauldron to help the fondant stick.

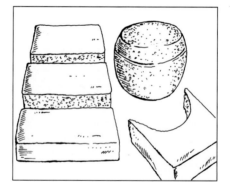

5 Spread butter cream in the curve of the remaining cake half and place at the bottom of the cauldron. As shown above.

6 Cut a slight curve on one of the long sides of each of the 3 cakes so they will fit snugly against the cauldron as the witch's body. Stick them together with butter cream and place them against the cauldron.

7 To shape the witch's body, trim both sides, slicing downwards at an angle, leaving 2.5 cm (1 inch) width at the top for the shoulders. Trim the back to round it off. Spread a thin layer of butter cream all over the witch's body.

8 Measure round the widest part of the cauldron with a length of cotton. Roll out 375g (13oz) of the black fondant icing until it is the same width as the cotton measure, then wrap round the cauldron, leaving the top uncovered. Tuck in the edges by the witch and trim the top and bottom. Roll out some of the black fondant trimmings and use to cover the witch's chest. Roll the remaining black fondant into a thick sausage shape the same length as the cotton measure. Using a little egg white or gum arabic, stick the fondant round the top of the cauldron as the rim.

9 With about a quarter of the black modelling fondant, model the arms. Gently push a skewer into the end of each arm and pull downwards to make the sleeves. Bend the arms slightly, then stick in place with a little egg white.

10 To model the witch's head, roll two-thirds of the green modelling fondant into a ball shape, then pinch the chin to make it pointed. With a cocktail stick, gently roll the chin a little flat, pushing upwards to make a ridge you can pinch out to make the nose. If you have difficulty with this, you can easily model and stick on a nose instead. Roll 2 tiny balls for the nose and chin warts. Paint egg white on to one of the skewers, then push into the witch's head, leaving 2.5 cm (1 inch) above the head to support the hat later. Push the skewer into the body until her head rests on the top of the cake.

11 Measure the length and width of the witch's back with 2 pieces of cotton thread and place these on the rolled out mauve fondant. Using the 2 cotton measures as a guide, cut out the cloak and wrap it round the witch's back.

12 Push the second skewer into the cauldron at a slight angle near the base of the sleeves for the broomstick handle. To model the hands, roll the remaining green modelling fondant into 2 balls. Flatten the ends slightly and make 4 cuts in each hand for the fingers. Pinch and pull each finger until they are long. Paint a little egg white or gum arabic on to the sleeves and the broomstick and stick the hands in place, wrapping the fingers round the broomstick.

13 Roll out the mauve modelling fondant and cut an oblong measuring 5 x 7 cm (2 x 3 inches). With a sharp knife,

indent the lines for the hair. Cut out a small oblong from either side to mark the fringe and wrap the hair round the back of the head, joining the fringe at the front.

14 With the white modelling fondant, roll 2 tiny balls for the witch's eyes and stick in place with a little egg white. Roll out and cut an oblong for the spell book pages and press a cocktail stick in the middle to mark between the pages. Set aside to dry.

15 Model the cat's tail and paws for inside the cauldron with small pieces of the black modelling fondant and set aside to dry. To make the hat, cut a 5 cm (2 inch) circle out of the remaining black modelling fondant and stick on top of the head through the skewer, then roll a cone shape and cut the bottom flat. Stick on with a little egg white or gum arabic and bend the top of the hat slightly to make it look floppy. Cut a small strip of fondant and wrap round the base as the hat band.

16 With the brown modelling fondant, roll out sausage shapes in varying sizes and mark lines with a sharp knife to resemble logs and sticks for the fire. Place round the base of the cauldron.

17 Roll out the mauve fondant trimmings and place the spell book pages on top. Cut round the white pages and set aside to dry.

18 Place the white royal icing in a greaseproof paper piping bag without a nozzle and snip the top to make quite a large opening. Squeeze the royal icing into the cauldron, swirling it to the edges until the surface is covered. Before the icing dries, put in the cat's paws and tail made earlier.

19 Pipe the flames with a star or shell nozzle and a greaseproof paper piping bag filled with a red royal icing on one side and egg yellow icing on the

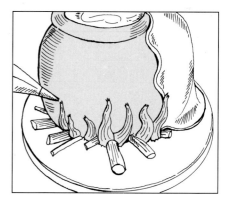

other side. Pipe the flames in an upward motion, pulling off sharply at the top to make them pointed.

20 Pipe the cobwebs with the No. 2 nozzle and the black royal icing. Pipe 4 lines 'criss-cross'. For the loops, start piping from the centre and work outwards in a circular motion. The spiders are made by piping 2 bulbs of royal icing together, one larger than the other. The legs are piped starting from the body and moving upwards, then sweeping the piping bag sharply down.

21 Sprinkle the silver snowflake lustre powder into the cauldron and on to the cobwebs. Leave the cake to dry for at least 8 hours, or overnight.

22 With the black food colouring pen, draw the eyes, eyebrows and wicked grin. Draw the writing on the spell book with the red food colouring pen. Stick the spell book on to the edge of the cauldron with a little egg white or gum arabic.

Teddy in a Lorry

A party with lots of colourful balloons and this cake 'centre stage' will make any small child's birthday a day to remember.

You will need:

1 quick mix cake (size 2)
1.35kg (3lb) fondant icing
75g (3oz) modelling fondant
yellow, blue and red food colouring paste
400g (14oz) butter cream
egg white or gum arabic
black food colouring pen

Equipment:

5-6 cocktail sticks
30 cm (12 inch) hexagonal cake board
ruler
5 cm (2 inch) and 4 cm (1½ inch) plain circle cutters
fine paintbrush
small, medium and large rose petal cutters

Colour:

Fondant icing: 450g (1lb) yellow, 450g (1lb) blue, 450g (1lb) red
Modelling fondant: 75g (3oz) yellow

1 Cover the cake board with 375g (13oz) of the yellow fondant icing and leave to dry.

2 Slice the top off the cake so it is completely flat.

3 Cut the cake into 3 pieces, 2 measuring 11 x 20 cm (4½ x 8 inches) and 1 measuring 7 x 20 cm (3 x 8 inches). Place the 2 larger cakes one on top of the other. Cut 2.5 cm (1 inch) off the shorter end of the remaining cake then cut exactly in half. Trim the top of one half to make the pointed roof, then put the 2 smaller cakes one on top of the other. Place the roof cake on the lorry cake as a guide, then cut a small hole in front of the roof where teddy is going to sit, measuring 2.5 x 6 cm (1 x 2½ inches) and 1 cm (½ inch) in depth.

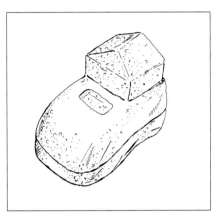

4 Cut away the front of the lorry so it slopes down and trim the sides to lose the sharp angles. Trim a little all round the base of the cake for the fondant icing to tuck under, as above.

5 Sandwich the 2 lorry cakes and the 2 roof cakes with butter cream.

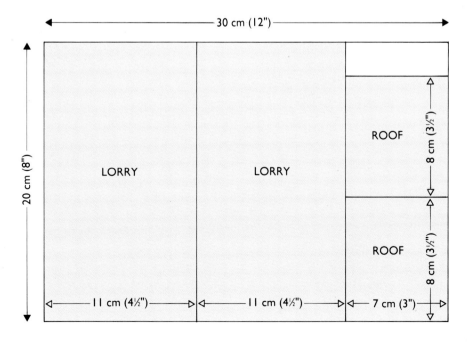

6 Spread a thin layer of butter cream all over the cakes to help the fondant stick and to seal the cake to prevent crumbs.

7 Roll out the blue fondant icing and cover the lorry cake. Push the icing gently into the space for teddy and using your thumb and forefinger, gently pinch up a windscreen in the front. Trim and tuck under round the base, then lift the cake gently on to the cake board. Mark the lines for the doors on either side with a sharp knife, then place the roof cake on top.

8 Roll out 275g (10oz) of the red fondant icing and cut pieces to fit all the sides of the roof. Gently indent the lines with the ruler and carefully place on the cake. Then cut a piece measuring 8 x 15 cm (3^1/$_2$ x 6 inches) for the top of the roof and gently indent the lines with the ruler. Place on top of the cake, letting it overlap equally on all sides.

9 With the remaining red fondant and the 5 cm (2 inch) circle cutter, cut out 4 wheels about 1 cm (^{1}/$_2$ inch) thick and stick in place with a little egg white or gum arabic.

10 With the remaining yellow fondant icing and the 4 cm (1^1/$_2$ inch) circle cutter, cut out 4 centres for the wheels and stick in place. Model 4 tiny balls for the hubcaps, and 2 headlights. Roll out a little fondant and cut out a grille for the front of the lorry, marking the lines with the ruler, as above.

11 With the blue fondant trimmings, make 4 mudguards, 2 door handles and the front and back bumpers. Stick in place with a little egg white or gum arabic.

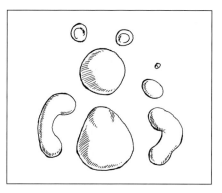

12 With 25g (1oz) of the yellow modelling fondant, roll a ball for teddy's body. Roll a slightly smaller ball for the head. Model the ears, arms and nose, then stick in place with a little egg white or gum arabic. Mark teddy's smile with a cocktail stick.

13 With the blue fondant trimmings, make a scarf 5 cm (2 inches) long and frill the ends. Wrap round teddy's neck. Model teddy's cap and stick in place.

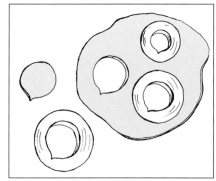

14 Roll out the red and yellow fondant trimmings and cut out balloon shapes with the rose petal cutters; stick in place on the lorry.

15 Leave the cake to dry for at least 8 hours, or overnight.

16 With the black food colouring pen, draw teddy's eyes and the balloon strings.

Alternative designs:

Another way of presenting this cake would be to model a different animal sitting in the front of the car. You could try a rabbit with an alert expression and his ears standing up proud, or a tabby cat with a lovely curling tail coming out of the side of the seat, or you could even try a small field mouse! Of course, you can ring the changes just as easily by colouring the cake in pretty pastel shades.

Right: Teddy in a lorry

Blue Bunny

This cuddly bunny rabbit has a lovely soft texture making him almost too good to eat!

You will need:

5 Madeira cakes (size 3, size 4, size 5, size 6)
700g (1lb 9oz) fondant icing
yellow, blue, black, orange and green food colouring paste
1.35kg (3lb) butter cream
egg white or gum arabic

Equipment:

5-6 cocktail sticks
25 cm (10 inch) round cake board
skewer
round ended knife
fork
fine paintbrush
sharp knife

Colour:

Fondant icing: 275g (10oz) pale yellow, 300g (11oz) blue, 5g (¼oz) white, 5g (¼oz) black, 100g (3½oz) orange, 15g (½oz) green
Butter cream: 600g (1lb 5oz) pale yellow, 750g (1lb 11oz) blue

1 Cover the cake board with the pale yellow fondant and leave to dry.

2 Slice the tops off all the cakes so they are completely flat. Cut the mug cake in half to make 2 circles, then trim slightly to make oval shapes for the feet.

3 Place the large bowl cake on top of the 15 cm (6 inch) round cake. To mark the arms, make a cut about 1 cm (½ inch) deep, and continue to cut in a curving line down to the bottom of the bowl cake. Mark the back of the arm with a similar curving line, 5 cm (2 inches) behind the first line. Repeat this for the other arm.

4 Slice down the front, keeping the tummy area quite rounded, and trim round to the arms. Slice downwards at the back, keeping the bottom area rounded, then trim round to the arms.

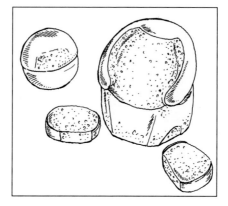

5 Slice out a piece of cake directly underneath each arm, then trim the base of the cake by about 5 mm (¼ inch) all the way round, cutting at an inwards angle, as shown above.

6 Trim the edges off the arms and any angles on the cake. Sandwich the 2 cakes with a quarter of the yellow butter cream, place the cake on the board.

7 Sandwich the 2 small bowl cakes together with yellow butter cream to make the head, and trim out a piece of cake to flatten the eye area. Place on top of the body and push the skewer down through the top of the head.

8 With a little of the yellow butter cream, stick the feet in position, then spread a thin layer of butter cream all over the cake to help the fondant stick and to seal the cake to prevent crumbs.

9 With the blue fondant icing, model two 50g (2oz) pieces into ears and press in position on top of the head, letting them bend naturally. Pad out the nose and hands with 25g (1oz) pieces of fondant. Cut another 25g (1oz) piece in half and press on for the cheeks. Model each leg with a 25g (1oz) piece of fondant and position on top of the feet. Roll a ball for the tail with the remaining fondant and stick in place.

10 Spread a thick layer of the blue butter cream over the feet and legs, then use a fork to mark the lines for the fur. Next, cover and mark the back, leaving the tail uncovered, then the chest area.

11 With the yellow butter cream, cover and mark the tummy area and the tail.

12 Spread some blue butter cream on the arms, marking the fur with a fork, then cover and mark the top of the head and the ears.

13 With the remaining yellow butter cream, cover the nose and cheek area, making the cheeks look very full and fluffy, as above.

14 Mark the mouth with a cocktail stick.

15 With the white fondant, model the eyes. Make the irises with the blue fondant trimmings, then with the black fondant, model the pupils and a nose.

Stick the irises and pupils on the eyes with a little egg white, then place the eyes and nose on the cake.

16 With one-third of the orange fondant, model a bow and put in place under bunny's chin. Roll the remaining orange fondant into a sausage shape, thinner at one end, for the carrot, then mark the lines with a sharp knife. Cut a leaf from the green fondant and stick on the end of the carrot with a little egg white or gum arabic.

17 Leave the cake to dry for at least 8 hours, or overnight.

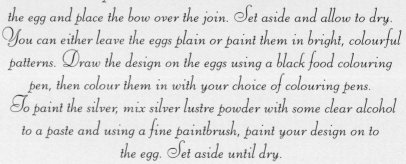

Alternative design:

To turn this pretty blue rabbit into an Easter bunny, make a few eggs instead of the carrot. Using 50g (2 oz) fondant icing, roll into an egg shape. Roll out some icing and cut strips for the ribbon and model small bows. Wrap the ribbon round the egg and place the bow over the join. Set aside and allow to dry. You can either leave the eggs plain or paint them in bright, colourful patterns. Draw the design on the eggs using a black food colouring pen, then colour them in with your choice of colouring pens. To paint the silver, mix silver lustre powder with some clear alcohol to a paste and using a fine paintbrush, paint your design on to the egg. Set aside until dry.

Christmas Toy Chest

A Christmas cake with a difference, here's a stunning centrepiece for the family table.

You will need:

1 rich fruit cake
900g (2lb) marzipan
1.1kg (2lb 7oz) fondant icing
650g (1lb 7oz) gelatine icing
800g (1lb 12oz) modelling fondant
red, golden brown, blue, yellow, green and brown food colouring paste
3 tablespoons apricot glaze
egg white or gum arabic
1-2 tablespoons clear alcohol, eg vodka or gin
silver lustre powder
red, blue, brown, green and yellow food colouring pens

Equipment:
8-10 cocktail sticks

30 cm (12 inch) square cake board
ruler
2 litre plastic soft drinks bottle
pastry brush
fine paintbrush
medium paintbrush
No. 4 piping nozzle
holly cutter
skewer (optional)

Colour:

Fondant icing: 450g (1lb) red, 650g (1lb 7oz) white
Gelatine icing: 650g (1lb 7oz) white
Modelling fondant: 75g (3oz) golden brown, 150g (5oz) white, 75g (3oz) blue, 75g (3oz) yellow, 200g (7oz) red, 200g (7oz) green

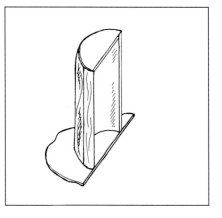

1 For the lid, roll out 350g (12oz) of the gelatine icing about 3 mm (1/8 inch) thick and cut an oblong measuring 14 x 22 cm (5½ x 8½ inches).

2 Working quickly and using a ruler, gently indent lines across the icing about 2 cm (3/4 inch) apart, then with a knife mark the wood bark pattern.

3 Dust the surface of the soft drinks bottle with icing sugar and lay the piece of gelatine icing over it. Leave to dry for at least 24 hours.

4 Cover the cake board with 350g (12oz) of the red fondant icing and leave to dry.

5 Cut the fruit cake in half and stick the 2 halves together, one on top of the other, with a thin layer of apricot glaze. To help the marzipan stick, brush the cake surface with the remaining apricot glaze. Roll out the marzipan 225g (8oz) at a time and measure and cut pieces to fit the sides and top of the fruit cake. Cover the front and back first, then the sides and finally the top. Leave to dry for 24 hours.

6 Carefully lift the dried lid away from the plastic bottle. Roll out 50g (2oz) of the gelatine icing and indent the lines and wood bark patterns as in step 1. Cut a clean, straight edge, then turn the icing over. Paint a little egg white or

gum arabic on to the curved ends of the treasure chest lid, then gently place one end on to the icing, lining up with the straight edge. Cut round to make the side of the lid, then repeat at the other end. Again, leave to dry for at least 24 hours, with the marked side up, as shown above.

7 Meanwhile, roll out the remaining red fondant icing, measure the top of the cake and cut a piece to fit. Brush the top of the cake with a little of the clear alcohol, then carefully stick the icing in place. Place the cake on the cake board.

8 Measure the front of the cake and with one-third of the white fondant icing, cut a piece to fit.

9 Indent lines across the icing with a ruler, then carefully mark the wood bark pattern with a knife. Brush the front of the cake with a little of the clear alcohol, then gently stick the icing in place. Do the same for the back and sides.

10 Place 1 tablespoon of water or alcohol into a bowl and add a small amount of brown food colouring paste, using the end of a cocktail stick. With the medium paintbrush, paint the toy chest and the lid, taking care not to splash the cake board. Set aside to dry.

11 With the remaining gelatine icing, cut 2 cm (³/₄ inch) and 5 mm (¹/₄ inch) wide strips for the metal trims and stick on to the toy chest and lid with a little egg white or gum arabic. Indent with the tip of the No. 4 piping nozzle to mark the rivets. Cut out the key lock with the end of the piping nozzle and cut the key hole with the tip. Cut out the 'L' shape corners and model 2 handles for the sides of the chest, then stick in place with a little egg white or gum arabic.

12 Mix the silver powder with a few drops of the clear alcohol and paint the strips, handles and key lock.

13 With the golden brown modelling fondant make the teddy. Roll a ball for the body and indent a line on the tummy with a cocktail stick. Roll a smaller ball for the head. Model the nose, ears, arms and feet and stick together with a little egg white or gum arabic. Leave to dry.

14 With the white modelling fondant, model 2 books with white covers wrapped round them, the middle of the drum, the kite, a square parcel and 8 building blocks.

15 With the blue modelling fondant, model the train, a square parcel and 2 sweets. To make the beach balls, roll 3 balls, one each of blue, yellow and red. Cut each ball into quarters and stick 4 alternate coloured quarters together with a little egg white or gum arabic. Make one blue and yellow ball and one red and yellow ball.

16 With the red modelling fondant, model 2 crackers, 2 parcels and 2 sweets. Model a tiny bow for the teddy and cut the trimmings for the toy train. Roll 15 tiny berries for the holly.

17 With the remaining yellow modelling fondant, model 3 sweets.

18 With the green modelling fondant, model 3 parcels. Cut 15 holly leaves and indent the vein with a cocktail stick. Model 6 tiny leaves for the crackers. Cut 2 circles for the top and bottom of the drum and cut a small square for the unwrapped present at the front of the toy chest.

19 With the remaining modelling fondant, cut the ribbon trims and bows for all the parcels. Make a rainbow ball by rolling scraps of red, yellow and blue fondant together until streaky. Leave all the toys to dry for 24 hours.

20 With the food colouring pens, draw the patterns on the kite, the lines on the drum, teddy's face, the book covers and the shapes on the building blocks.

21 Stick all the toys in place using a little egg white or gum arabic, placing teddy at the front to support the lid. You can use a skewer for extra stability, pushing it into the centre of the fruit cake for the lid to rest on.

22 With the red modelling fondant, roll a long thin sausage shape to fit the length of the toy chest and stick along the back behind all the toys. Paint a little egg white or gum arabic on to it, then put the lid in place, letting the back of the lid rest on the red strip and the front on teddy's head.

Alternative designs:

This Christmas toy chest also looks good filled with chocolates and sweets if you feel it will be too time-consuming to make all the toys. Another alternative, this time for a birthday, is a pirate treasure chest filled with foil-covered chocolate coins. For the above, use a skewer inserted in the middle of the cake to support the lid.

Note:

I recommend you start decorating this cake 3 weeks before it is needed to give you plenty of drying time.

Right: Christmas toy chest

Useful Suppliers and Addresses

Blue Ribbons Cakecraft Centre
110 Walton Road
East Molesey KT8 0HP
Tel: 081 941 1591

Blackburn's Cake Centre
108 Alexandra Drive
Surbiton KT5 9AG
Tel: 081 399 6875

Mary Jane's Pantry
60 Church Road
Ashford
Middlesex TW15 2TS
Tel: 0784 252904

Squires Kitchen
3 Waverley Lane
Farnham
Surrey GU9 8BB
Tel: 0252 734309

Felicity Clare
360 Leach Place
Walton Summit, Bamber Bridge
Preston
Lancashire PR5 8AR
Tel: 0772 628286

A Piece of Cake
18 Upper High Street
Thame
Oxfordshire
OX9 3EX
Tel: 0844 213428

Elizabeth David Cookshop
3 North Row
The Market
Covent Garden
London WC2 8RA
Tel: 071 836 9167

G. T. Culpitt & Son Ltd.
Culpitt House
Place Farm
Wheathamstead
Hertfordshire
AL4 8SB
Tel: 0582 834122

British Sugarcraft Guild
Wellington House
Messeter Place
Eltham
London
SE9 5DP
Tel: 081 859 6943

North America
Maid of Scandinavia
3244 Raleigh Avenue
Minneapolis
MN 55416

Wilton Enterprises Inc
2240 West 75th Street
Woodridge
Illinois 60517

Home Cake Artistry Inc
1002 North Central
Suite 511
Richardson
Texas 75080

Creative Tools Ltd.
3 Tannery Court
Richmond Hill
Ontario
Canada L4C 7V5

Australia
Australian National Cake Decorators'
Association
PO Box 321
Plympton SA5038

New Zealand
New Zealand Cake Decorators' Guild
Secretary Julie Tibble
78 Kirk Street
Otaki
Wellington

South Africa
South African Sugarcraft Guild
National Office
1 Tuzla Mews
187 Smit Street
Fairlan 2195

Index